Inner
Journeys

About the Author

Gloria Chadwick is a writer and teacher with more than thirty years of experience. Through her books and workshops, she has helped thousands of people learn how to meditate.

To Write to the Author

If you wish to contact the author or would like more information about this book, please write to the author in care of Llewellyn Worldwide and we will forward your request. Both the author and publisher appreciate hearing from you and learning of your enjoyment of this book and how it has helped you. Llewellyn Worldwide cannot guarantee that every letter written to the author can be answered, but all will be forwarded. Please write to:

Gloria Chadwick
%Llewellyn Worldwide
2143 Wooddale Drive, Dept. 0-7387-0898-4
Woodbury, Minnesota 55125-2989, U.S.A.

Please enclose a self-addressed stamped envelope for reply, or $1.00 to cover costs. If outside of the U.S.A., enclose an international postal reply coupon.

Many of Llewellyn's authors have websites with additional information and resources. For more information, please visit our website at http://www.llewellyn.com

Gloria Chadwick

Meditations
&
Visualizations

Inner Journeys

Llewellyn Publications
Woodbury, Minnesota

First Edition
First Printing, 2006

Book design by Steffani Chambers
Cover design by Lisa Novak
Cover art © 2006 by Digital Vision

Llewellyn is a registered trademark of Llewellyn Worldwide, Ltd.

Library of Congress Cataloging-in-Publication Data
Chadwick, Gloria.
  Inner journeys : meditations & visualizations / by Gloria Chadwick
    p. cm.
  ISBN-13: 978-0-7387-0898-0
  ISBN-10: 0-7387-0898-4
    1. Meditation. 2. Visualization. I. Title.

  BF637.M4C47 2006
  158.1'2—dc22   2006044719

Llewellyn Publications

A Division of Llewellyn Worldwide, Ltd.
2143 Wooddale Drive, Dept. 0-7387-0898-4
Woodbury, Minnesota 55125-2989, U.S.A.
www.llewellyn.com

Printed in the United States of America

Books by Gloria Chadwick

Discovering Your Past Lives

Spirituality & Self-Empowerment

Somewhere Over the Rainbow: A Soul's Journey Home

Soul Shimmers: Awakening Your Spiritual Self

Happy Ways to Heal the Earth

The Key To Self-Empowerment

Life is Just A Dream

Psychic Senses: How to Develop Your Innate Powers

Reincarnation and Your Past-Life Memories

This book is dedicated to Hannah,
my granddaughter.

Contents

Introduction

Inner Journeys originated from special journeys in my mind, secret places in my heart, and sacred spaces in my soul. It mirrors some of the meditations and guided visualizations in my classes and workshops, and in my previous books.

It is my sincere hope that the meditations in this book, in addition to being soothing and relaxing, and in some cases quite energizing, will help you open up your inner knowing to attain a higher level of awareness and insight, and will show you the spiritual symbolism and the magic in your everyday activities and experiences.

I hope they'll encourage and empower you on your path of self-discovery and aid you in remembering your spiritual knowledge and reawakening to your true spiritual self.

As you journey inside your mind with the images drawn from words, you'll be opening up many wonderful worlds within yourself that lead to other realms of reality, and you'll be exploring mystical mindscapes in a very special place within you.

While I've worded the meditations in an open way for you to experience and explore whatever comes into your mind in a unique and individual manner, and to interpret what you experience in your own way, several of them are designed to guide you in a specific direction and to achieve certain purposes.

Some of the meditations are short, offering a few descriptive sentences that provide the essence of the intended imagery, or they present several ideas and suggestions with a paragraph or two of general instructions that will inspire you to imagine and create your inner journey for yourself.

Rely on your mind to give you the images, thoughts, and feelings that will guide your self-exploration and discoveries. This is a very powerful way to open up your imagination and to see inside your inner knowing.

As you may notice in some of the meditations, the teacher in me slips out from time to time. This is most apparent in the suggestions and notes that I offer after a few of the meditations. Please accept these as other avenues to explore, if you choose, as you open up windows and doorways on your own.

In this way I honor the true teacher within me because I've shared my knowledge with you and shown you some ways to access your inner knowing—to learn ever so much more within yourself—and to remember your own spiritual knowledge.

I'd like to think that you will allow the meditations in this book to shine a light on your path that will be helpful to you in finding and illuminating the truth for yourself. Your true teacher is within, and you find your own truth by looking within yourself and discovering what is real for you by following your feelings.

Your mind is waiting to show you many magical and mystical worlds within yourself. When you take the time to relax and be quiet— to be natural, to be who you really are, to just *be*—you're able to enter a meditative frame of mind and to easily direct your attention into yourself. There you can listen to your thoughts and allow your feelings to speak clearly. You can look at what you hear and know the true awareness of your spirit.

Take some time for yourself and relax. Read through the meditations slowly, one at a time, and savor them. Allow the words to form into images and to open up thoughts and feelings inside your mind as they draw you into a special, magical world within yourself. Then close your eyes and imagine that you're there. It's as easy as believing it to be so.

Let your mind be your guide through the wonderful world of your inner images. Somewhere inside yourself, you'll touch your true feelings and rediscover the magic of the real you—the magic of your inner spiritual self. Listen quietly and you'll hear a voice that whispers to you—your inner voice that's real and true, the voice that always speaks the truth.

Part One Introduction To Meditation

Meditation takes on many forms and expressions. Meditation can be so much more than sitting quietly or chanting. Meditation provides you a direct pathway into your subconscious mind, into the knowing awareness you have within yourself.

The meditations inside this book are as soft as the silence that flows in rhythm with the gentle stream of your spirit. The words are like poetry in motion, drawing beautiful images into your mind and creating magical, mystical worlds in your heart.

Inner Journeys offers you a peaceful, quiet, tranquil time to tune into your inner self and your soul. The meditations invite you to travel on the wings of your spirit to explore the many multi-dimensional realms within you and the worlds of the universe around you.

By taking a few moments to meditate, you can tune into who you really are; you can touch and fully experience your essence. Your heart, mind, and soul will show you all the joys and wonders within you and the many magical, mystical worlds that your spirit travels.

The Many Ways to Meditate

There are many ways to meditate and many methods of meditation. You've probably practiced some of these in one way or another. All forms of meditation are wonderful and have two things in common: physical relaxation and focusing your complete attention and awareness into your subconscious mind.

Meditation can range anywhere from lightly exploring your imagination to deeply experiencing your awareness. The following list is not comprehensive or all-inclusive; it briefly describes various ways to meditate and offers some metaphysical uses and everyday applications of meditation.

Active

Taking long, peaceful walks through the woods or along the beach, or in another natural setting where you feel comfortable and at ease, to tune into nature and to be at one with the world around you and in touch with the world within you, with the naturalness of yourself.

Being in nature—in a beautiful, natural place—replenishes and rejuvenates you, and has a wonderful calming effect on both your body and your mind. This is because nature is in harmony with itself and inspires that same feeling within you.

Breathing

Briefly stretching your body and breathing deeply as you take a moment or two for yourself. It provides a change of mind and focus of awareness.

You probably do this several times during the day, and you also do it automatically and naturally every time you wake up (unless you jump up out of bed, roused by the intrusive sound of an alarm clock). You also do this every night, very often unconsciously, as you go into the early stages of sleep.

Chanting

Slowly repeating a specific syllable or word, usually the word "OM" (pronounced ohm) or "HU" (pronounced hue) to clear and calm your conscious mind.

The vibration of the word focuses your mind and centers your attention within yourself. It also helps to put you in touch with a higher power, with the essence of your spiritual self. In addition, people will often burn incense at the same time to create a spiritual mood.

Guided Imagery

The imagery of words draws pictures and creates scenes in your mind as the meditation guides you into a gentle feeling of peaceful relaxation for quiet contemplation and reflection, and/or the pleasure and enjoyment of going within your subconscious to open up and explore whatever the words inspire as they lead you into wherever your mind takes you.

Guided imagery also serves specific purposes; it can help you to relieve stress, achieve goals, facilitate healing, and open up the magical, mystical power of your mind. (See Visualization. These topics are also covered in more detail in the next chapter.)

Mindfulness

Being completely aware of what you're doing and where you're at. This keeps you centered and connected with your current emotions and experiences.

By focusing on your breathing and placing your full attention into yourself and your surroundings, you become present in the very real moment of here and now. It allows you to be happy at all times, to see the beauty and experience the wonder in all things, and to enjoy life with the simplicity of a child.

(Thich Nhat Hanh, a Vietnamese monk and Zen master, has written many books on mindfulness meditation. My favorite is *Peace Is Every Step*.)

Musings

To muse about something is to pay full attention to it and to ponder it deeply. It is a synonym for meditation. Many creative people, such as writers, artists, and musicians, often listen to the muse in their mind to receive inspiration for their creative endeavors.

Prayer

Directing your attention toward a divine essence, being, or higher power that you perceive to be outside of yourself, such as the Universe, God, Buddha, or an angel or spiritual guide. It is most often used as a channel for requests or to receive answers, insights, and assistance from higher sources.

Prayer focuses your desires, thoughts, and feelings. It also helps to put you in touch with your divine, inner spiritual essence, and serves the purpose of guiding you within to your own higher power.

Relaxation

Simply sitting in a comfortable chair or stretching out on a couch to quietly think your thoughts, or to just breathe and be, is a wonderful form of meditation.

Sipping a cup of tea or drinking coffee can warm your hands as well as your heart, as you allow your conscious mind to relax, to free itself from the cares, worries, and negative thoughts of the day as you ease the tension from your body. This helps you to quietly relax and to gently calm your mind.

Reveries

Thinking, imagining, creating, and seeing various situations and scenarios happening in your mind. Similar to unguided visualizations and daydreams, where your mind wanders into other realms of reality, reveries allow your mind to meander through the myriad paths that your feelings take you on as your imagination shows you the different possible and probable ways your experiences could play out.

They offer you the opportunity to quietly think about and to ponder your thoughts; to open up your insights, ideas, and intuition; to reflect on past experiences; to look into and explore present events; or to contemplate future plans, dreams, and goals.

Reveries are sometimes used to help counteract boredom by empty-mindedly gazing out the window, or zoning out during a dull lecture or business meeting, or imagining yourself in another place doing something enjoyable.

While getting "lost" in a mindless place or changing your perceptual awareness by going somewhere else more appealing in your thoughts serves a purpose by allowing you to escape reality for a few moments, reveries do much more than that.

They offer you insightful and intuitive mind trips. By analyzing and interpreting their content, they very often—sometimes literally and sometimes symbolically—give you answers to questions you've been considering or wondering about and puzzling over. At times, they simply offer your conscious mind a much-needed respite from stress or anxiety.

Shamanic Journeying

Traveling into and through non-ordinary realities, used primarily by indigenous people to travel into the higher and lower worlds for physical and spiritual healing, as well as to enter astral and ethereal realms for insight and spiritual knowledge.

It is also used to journey through time and space to visit other realities for many spiritual purposes, such as soul retrieval, to speak with another person's heart, or to connect with past or future selves or events to see and recreate the past in a new way, or to design and alter the future.

Shamans often connect with the spirits of nature and call upon their power animals, other allies and spiritual entities to request their protection and assistance, or to guide them in achieving whatever they are doing. This is usually accompanied by drumming and chanting, dancing and ritual.

Many people use quiet meditation or imagery to achieve the same thing: to enter an altered state of consciousness to access their natural, inborn healing abilities, and to be more in tune with their spiritual essence. Many times we go on shamanic journeys in our dreams and astral projections.

Transcendental

Elevating your mind above the mundane physical world to detach yourself and your emotions, and to remove your consciousness from it. This cleanses and focuses your mind, raising it to a higher plane by emptying it and clearing out negativity as you let go of conscious, trivial thoughts and feelings. The mind is perfectly calm, centered, and tranquil, bringing a deep, relaxing feeling of peace.

Visualization

Seeing with your mind's eye, using imagery to clearly visualize yourself doing or achieving something first in your mind to help you manifest it in your life. An example is athletes who use visualization to see themselves excelling in their sports by focusing their awareness and picturing the way a certain scene or event will happen to help them achieve their desired result.

Another example is visualizing a tangible, touchable goal to help you attain it, such as buying a house or a new car. It can also be used to help you achieve an intangible goal or purpose, such as an emotional shift where you change your perspectives and perceptions, and thereby alter your feelings. Visualization also has tremendous value and benefit in healing, and can bring about seemingly "miraculous" cures.

It is similar to mind projection, where you project your awareness into a past, present, or future scene to help you clearly understand it, or to create it in the way you desire. When used for manifesting, it is always a good idea to keep the thought in mind that whatever you desire will happen for the highest good of all involved.

You unconsciously use visualization, and your feelings and thought energy, every day in every moment and experience to create your own reality. Conscious visualization allows you to be more focused and aware of what you are doing.

Yoga and T'ai Chi

These Eastern forms of meditation consist of slow, gentle stretches and body postures, combined with rhythmic breathing and conscious awareness of your body, mind, and spirit working together as a unified whole.

The exercises and movements harmonize body and mind, and balance both the physical and spiritual flow of energy within your body. They focus your awareness, allowing you to achieve centered calmness and clarity of mind. These and other forms of Eastern exercise and philosophy are also referred to as meditation in motion.

Zen

Meditating on nothing or emptiness by completely clearing and stilling your conscious mind. You focus your attention on your breathing to bring inner peace and stillness of mind. This can be very calming, relaxing, and peaceful, as well as spiritually nourishing and rejuvenating in stressful times. This is also referred to as sitting.

If a conscious thought enters your awareness and attempts to interrupt you, you acknowledge it as merely a thought and gently let it go, without attaching any feelings to it or giving it any importance, thinking about it, or dwelling on it. You simply allow your mind to be quiet.

There are many ways to meditate and many ways to use meditation. One way is not better than another; they're simply different from each other. Many of the forms are similar and tend to meld together, merging into aspects of one another.

You can meditate using some combination of all of the above at various times, depending on your individual desires, needs, preferences, lifestyle, and circumstances. Just go with the flow. Whatever works for you and helps you to incorporate meditation into your daily life is the best way for you to meditate.

Principles and Purposes

The many physical and spiritual values and benefits of meditating are far-reaching and multi-faceted. Meditation can help you in any area of your life that you desire. The manner and many various ways in which you can use it are unlimited. The scope and power of your mind and your imagination are absolutely awesome.

The first step to meditating is just simply relaxing. As you relax, your brain waves synchronize their pattern from your everyday, waking, conscious level (beta) to a subtle, subconscious, and more aware level of mind (alpha). As you enter a more aware level of mind, you create and enjoy a greater positive attitude and a better frame of mind.

Relaxing also automatically and naturally promotes health and harmony in body, mind, and spirit. By relaxing your body and allowing your conscious mind to become calm and quiet, physical changes occur within your body that relate directly to your health and well-being. You reduce and eliminate stress, tension, and fatigue. Your breathing and heart rate slow to a natural, peaceful rhythm, which affects your internal organs and your nervous system in gentle, healing ways.

The holistic value of meditation and its effect on mind-body connections are intricately interrelated. When you use self-guided imagery or a guided visualization in an aware, focused, and directed manner, you greatly expand and enhance your body's own natural ability to heal itself.

As you begin to meditate by opening up and expanding your inner awareness, you open avenues of self-discovery and expression. You open your receptivity to ideas, images, and insights that in turn open up your intuition and influence your creativity. You open up your natural abilities to visualize—to see with your mind's eye—and to intuitively feel with your inner senses.

Meditation is wonderfully uplifting. It can bring your spirits up and change your mood and perceptions if you're feeling stressed out, sad or depressed, discouraged or worried. It's a great way to take care of the blahs and is a super five-minute refresher that rejuvenates you and improves your attitude.

Meditating can help you to recognize deep and powerful emotions that may be affecting you unconsciously, and to bring them into your conscious mind. It offers a gentle, nurturing way to look into negative and/or traumatic feelings and memories. It helps you get in touch with, tune into, and understand your true feelings.

Meditation is self-empowering. It allows you to go within yourself to open up and reclaim your own personal power to achieve self-growth and to make clear, conscious choices and changes in your life that will help you to move in a positive direction. It allows you to be in charge of your life and to create the circumstances you desire.

Meditating helps you to become more aware of your inner self and to recognize your spiritual self. It opens a window to your inner knowing and to your awareness of your true nature; it helps you remember and rediscover your spiritual knowledge by inviting you to visit sacred spaces in your soul.

Meditation offers you spiritual enlightenment. You can use meditation to explore multidimensional realms within your mind to give you insights and perspectives that can provide you with alternative avenues of perception to clearly see into and understand the spiritual symbolism of your experiences, and to really know what's inside your soul.

Most of all, meditation offers you the freedom to be exactly who you are, to accept yourself completely as you are, and to just simply experience being yourself in a natural, carefree, joyous state of mind.

There are three types of meditation presented in this book. The first type is unguided meditation—simply relaxing and entering a quiet, still, peaceful place in your mind. This offers you several options: to think about nothing at all, to just relax and refresh yourself, to center and focus yourself in the present moment, or to calm your conscious mind to relieve stress.

To enter and be in an unguided meditation, simply focus your attention on your breathing to relax you as you simultaneously quiet and clear your conscious mind. (See the Rhythm of Relaxing meditation in the following section, page 14.)

To open up and experience the images inside your mind to see where they'll take you and what they'll show you, just relax and let it happen; go with the flow. Let go of any preconceived ideas or feelings and open up your mind to receive your awareness from within. Your inner imagery and insights will show you what you need to see.

Another way to experience this is to open this book at random and go with the flow. Allow the meditation you've chosen, seemingly by chance, to resonate within you. You'll find that your intuition has opened to the page that holds the answer to a question you may have, or a solution to a problem you might be puzzling over.

Maybe the meditation will provide you with information you need to know, or show you something that will be helpful or beneficial to you in some area of your life. It may address a particular concern you might have, or it may spark an idea or insight that offers you what you most need at the moment.

The second type is self-guided, where you meditate on whatever you choose. You originate and create the images, and design and direct your own meditation. You can explore and experience anything you want; you can go wherever you choose in your mind, and you can achieve any purpose you desire. This is a wonderful way to access your intuition and inner knowing, and to open up and expand the power of your mind.

The third type is guided visualization, which leads you in a definite direction and is intended to achieve specific results. The meditations and visualizations in this book are worded to be interactive, and either gently guide you or provide you with the beginnings of a self-guided meditation. They offer you images and suggestions to get you started, then they let your mind guide you and show you what is within.

Whatever you experience in your meditation will be filtered and colored by your frame of reference. You're a unique, special individual, and your mind will offer you the images and insights that are most meaningful and appropriate for you.

Adapt the meditations and visualizations in this book to suit your lifestyle and to fit your frame of mind. Follow your own feelings, depending on what direction you choose to pursue and on what you feel like doing. Be open to seeing and experiencing what your mind shows you.

Meditating is similar to lucid dreaming, where you clearly and consciously know that you're dreaming, and you can change and/or direct the dream. Because this occurs simultaneously on a conscious and a subconscious level, you can easily understand and interpret the imagery in your meditations.

Since some people may not be able to clearly remember or completely understand their dreams, meditating can also help to open a doorway into their dreams because there are no confusing cobwebs or misty bits and pieces of dream imagery floating through their minds or zipping in and out of their awareness so quickly that they barely have time to see the image, much less understand and interpret it.

One of the benefits of consciously meditating is that your nighttime dreams will become clearer and you'll remember more of the details, as well as being able to better understand and clearly interpret the symbolism and meaning of your dreams.

The more you meditate, the more adept you will become at entering more aware levels of mind—whether you're asleep or awake—where you can access ever-higher levels of awareness, and where you can reawaken to your spiritual self and attain enlightenment within yourself by remembering your inner knowledge and recognizing the true nature of your soul.

Enjoy the meditations, guided visualizations, and self-guided imageries in this book. Allow them to inspire you to explore many other areas of awareness within yourself as you reach into, through, and above realms of reality and stretch your imagination and mind into deeper dimensions of your true spiritual self.

Rhythm of Relaxing

There's an art to meditating—to getting inside your subconscious mind to that still, quiet, peaceful place within you, to that spiritual realm of knowing awareness where you can reconnect with your inner self and reawaken to your true essence—and it's easy to do.

All you have to do is breathe naturally, relax your body as you calm your conscious mind, and allow images to form inside the wonderful world of your imagination and inner knowing.

If you're new to meditation, you'll probably experience conscious mind chatter. The chatter is merely a distraction that goes something like this: "Omigod, I'm overdrawn at the bank and that check is going to bounce. I forgot to make an appointment with the dentist. I have to go to the grocery store to get milk and bread. Work was awful and it's going to be even worse tomorrow. I should call so-and-so, and I have to do this, that, and the other, etc., so on and so forth . . ." Just chatter, mostly about mundane matters, info you can listen to when you're not centering your attention on the magic of meditation and opening up youre mind's awareness.

If a thought that sounds like conscious chatter runs through your mind, just watch it run by; let it drift in and out. If it's important for you to be aware of right now, it will sit there in the center of your mind and make faces at you until you pay attention to it. Gently focus your awareness on your breathing; allow your breathing to relax your body and to quiet the chatter as you direct your attention inward.

Stretch out on a couch or sit in a comfortable chair that completely supports your neck and back. Begin to relax your body with a few deep breaths to calm and clear your mind. As you're breathing in, imagine that you're inhaling positive, relaxing feelings, allowing a gentle feeling of relaxation to softly flow into and through you.

As you're breathing out, imagine that you're exhaling negative thoughts and feelings, letting go of all cares, worries, and problems, releasing your thoughts from your everyday experiences as you ease all the tension and tightness from your body.

As your conscious mind becomes calm and quiet, and your body becomes more comfortable and relaxed, you tune out the physical world for a time as you tune into a subtle, more aware, inner level of mind.

By directing and focusing your attention inward, you begin to see and sense your inner images as you open up your subconscious awareness and enter into a meditative, more aware frame of mind. But for now, for the moment, just relax and let your thoughts go. Focus on your breathing and simply feel a gentle flow of relaxation begin to drift softly into and through your body.

Imagine that you're breathing in a peaceful, pure, cleansing white light that calms your mind, that heals and harmonizes every part of your body as it gently circulates within and through you.

Breathe in this wonderful image and feeling. Allow it to calm, quiet, and clear your conscious mind, and to softly and naturally relax your body. Breathe in this wonderfully beneficial white light to help you open up your subconscious awareness—your inner knowing.

This image and feeling is very special because your body and your mind resonate naturally with the spiritual/universal essence and vibrations of white light.

Breathe. Just breathe. You can interact with and influence your level of relaxation simply through your breathing. Allow your breathing to relax your body, to calm and quiet your conscious mind, and to open up your inner awareness.

Allow your breathing, and the image and feeling of white light, to bring you into a peaceful place within yourself. As you breathe, listen to your body feelings. Take your time and go slowly, seeing and feeling and completely experiencing every image and sensation, honoring and accepting what you experience.

Relaxing your body, opening up your subconscious mind, and focusing your attention and awareness inward is a gentle, flowing process. It's as easy and natural as breathing.

As you take another deep breath in, completely stretch out on your couch or in your comfortable chair. Breathe some more. Read through the following relaxation suggestions, then close your eyes and get into the rhythm of relaxing.

As you're breathing, allow a soft, easy, wonderful, peaceful feeling of relaxation to gently and naturally replace body tension. Allow all the muscles and nerves and tissues—every part of your body—to relax from the top of your head all the way down through the tips of your toes.

Feel this calming, soothing, gentle feeling of relaxation flow deeply down into and through your body, within every part of you, beginning at the top of your head.

Imagine this feeling and your breathing as a very gentle wave of motion that flows slowly and softly into and through you, descending gradually through all the muscles in your forehead and your face, relaxing the muscles around your eyes, your mouth, and your jaw.

Continue to breathe naturally as you allow your breathing to relax you even more.

Let this very peaceful, calming, soothing feeling of relaxation flow slowly down into and through your neck and your shoulders, gently easing all the tension, letting it drift away, replacing it with a soft, natural feeling of relaxation that flows all the way down into and through your back, vertebra by vertebra, loosening and letting go of all the tension and tightness from the muscles in your back.

As this gentle feeling of relaxation simultaneously flows softly down into and through your chest and abdomen, and as your stomach muscles relax, you'll notice that your breathing becomes deeper and slows to a more regular, natural rhythm that is in harmony with your level of relaxation.

Now that you're feeling much more relaxed, maybe you'd like to move around a bit, to readjust your position and get even more comfortable. Take a moment to stretch and then relax even more deeply, now that you've let go of all the tension and tightness from your face and jaw, your neck and shoulders, and from your back, chest, and abdomen.

Sinking deeper into the couch or comfortable chair, letting it completely support you, continue to allow this peaceful, gentle, soft, easy feeling of relaxation to flow slowly and naturally down from your shoulders into and through your arms, elbows, wrists, hands, and fingers.

Continue to breathe naturally, feeling the gentle, harmonious, healing essence of white light circulate softly through your body. You feel so deeply relaxed now. Peaceful. Quiet. Soothed, as the soft, easy feeling of relaxation continues to flow gently down from your stomach into and through your hips and your legs, all the way down into and through your thighs, knees, calves, ankles, feet, and toes.

You're so comfortable and relaxed, feeling perfectly content and in tune with yourself, in harmony with your body and your mind. Enjoy your calm, quiet, peaceful feeling of relaxation for a while. Just breathe and be happy. Enjoy the warm, pleasant feeling of just being.

Learning the Language of Your Mind

Your subconscious speaks to you by showing you symbols and imagery, and talks to you through your thoughts and feelings, using pictures instead of words; it's the language of your mind. The thoughts you hear, the feelings you sense, and the pictures you see in your mind originate in your imagination—the world of your inner images.

The following mind-opening meditation is a self-guided visualization to help you gently stretch your mind and open up your imagination as you see the spiritual symbolism of your soul and learn the language of your mind. Take your time inside your mind—inside your imagination—to completely explore, experience, and enjoy every part of this meditation.

Before you begin, think about this analogy for a few minutes. Your subconscious mind—your inner awareness—is like a bud that's growing into a very beautiful flower. Allow it to grow at its own rate. Nurture it with care and loving attention. As a bud, it needs time to develop and open up, to flower and bloom, and to flourish and grow into a beautiful garden.

Start your meditation by relaxing and breathing. Enter into a calm, peaceful, quiet place within you. Ease and erase the tension and tightness from your body. Clear your thoughts and feelings from your everyday experiences and open yourself up to experiencing the magic inside your mind.

Now, imagine and create a yellow rosebud in your mind. Take your time; be very descriptive and detailed in your visualization. Feel and sense this rosebud with every part of your mind and your imagination. Use all your physical senses in an inner way to see, hear, smell, touch, and taste the vibrations and energies of this beautiful yellow rosebud. Breathe in and be the essence of the rosebud inside you.

As you imagine and create the rosebud, clearly visualize the image; see the thought of it in your mind. The thought itself will draw a picture for you. Perhaps this meditation will inspire a memory of when you saw a beautiful yellow rosebud, or another image, thought, or feeling will appear in your mind, or you may just get a sense of the rosebud.

Maybe you'll remember when someone sent you roses and what they looked and smelled like, and what they felt like as you gently touched the petals, or you'll remember when you had a single rose in a vase in your home or on your desk at work.

Perhaps you'll recall the last time you saw and smelled a rose when you were outside, and you'll also become aware of what the weather was like, and all the many other sights and sounds around you as you thoroughly employ all your senses.

Perhaps the meditation will bring forth an image of a rosebush in your own garden that is beginning to bud and open up. As you meditate on what you see, sense, or feel, it will begin to move, to flow with the momentum of your meditation. Perhaps you'll see a scene with several images that move and change as you become more involved with and aware of them.

Completely open yourself up to totally experiencing—with all your physical and inner senses, with every part of your mind and your imagination, and on all levels of your awareness—what your subconscious shows you. Accept whatever you see.

By accepting the pictures that your mind offers you, you open a channel of communication between your conscious and subconscious minds. The images you see—the thoughts, ideas, and insights you become aware of—and the feelings you experience will be meaningful for you in a very special way.

When you're done with this meditation, and while everything you experienced is clear and vivid in your mind, take some time to quietly think about and to reflect on the images you saw, the thoughts you heard, and the feelings you became aware of.

This quiet time after a meditation allows you to bring your inner knowing and subconscious awareness into your conscious mind, where you can fully understand it on all levels of your awareness. This quiet time to flow the images and insights into your conscious mind also allows you to bring more of what you experienced on your inner journey into your conscious awareness.

You might want to write down what you saw and felt. Completely describe the images you saw in your mind, the thoughts you became aware of, and the feelings they brought forth. Define what they represent to you on an inner, feeling level. This helps you to remember more of your meditation, to understand it better, and to incorporate and blend it into your physical consciousness.

If the images were blurry, or if you felt or sensed them more than you saw them, that's okay. Be clear and detailed in your descriptions of what you experienced. You've just said "hi" to your subconscious, and it responded by showing you images of your thoughts and feelings.

Sometimes people have a little difficulty visualizing—seeing with their mind's eye. They sense or feel their images and thoughts. There's really no right or wrong way to do things. Whatever way and however you experience meditation is the right way for you. Maybe you just need to redevelop your inner sense of sight, or maybe your inner sense of feeling is stronger. Both are important in meditating and visualizing.

Visualization is the ability to see scenes and images inside your mind with your eyes closed. This is a natural ability, but if you have trouble in seeing with your mind's eye, try this:

Look at a picture or an object of what you want to visualize. Concentrate your full attention on it. Take your time and notice all the details. Then close your eyes and recreate a picture of it in your mind or remember what it looks like.

With a little time and practice, you'll soon reactivate your inner sense of seeing. And keep this in mind: You already know how to visualize. You do it every night inside your dreams when you see the images.

It's just as important to open up and redevelop your inner sense of feeling—to sense what something feels like, or to sense what it looks like. This helps you learn to listen to yourself, to hear your inner voice and to become aware of your inner self, to read both your conscious and subconscious images, thoughts, and feelings clearly, and to trust the knowing you have within you.

It helps you to see both underneath and inside your experiences, whether you're meditating or just going about your daily activities, and to know what's really going on inside your mind as you open up your intuition and your awareness.

It's also helpful to completely immerse yourself in your meditations, to focus your full attention on them, and to go inside each image and feeling to see what your subconscious is showing you and saying to you. Become totally involved with your imagination to feel or sense what your images are really like, and what they represent to you.

This helps you understand the language of your mind and will also help you open up your imagination and develop your inner senses of seeing and feeling. Note any thoughts or ideas or insights that come to you when you're in a meditative frame of mind—a level of increased subconscious awareness.

At first you may think that you're making up what you experience, that you're playing with your imagination. This isn't true. What you're really doing is opening up your inner imagery and spiritual knowing, to see the truth within you. You're setting your subconscious mind free to show you what you already know, but may have allowed yourself to forget or to misunderstand.

Learn to trust your feelings and what comes into your mind as a genuine reflection of your inner knowing by accepting whatever you experience as real and true.

To understand the thoughts and feelings you've become aware of, the insights you've received, or the imagery you've seen and sensed, and what they represent to you, ask your subconscious—your inner self—for the interpretations and answers.

Let them come into your conscious mind. Ponder them a bit; let them be gentle on your mind. By doing this, you'll open up your inner awareness even more; you'll gain a better understanding of what your subconscious is saying to you and a clearer understanding of what it is showing you.

Meditating helps you to open up your intuition and your imagination, to enter and explore the magical world of your inner images and spiritual knowing, to reconnect with your inner self and reunite with your spiritual self—the one who speaks to you through your thoughts, ideas, images, insights, and feelings—the one who whispers to you in your mind.

Your imagination is where you rediscover the real you, where you're totally free to simply be who you really are. It's where you find that very special, sacred part of you that is within every area of your life from the blah to the blissful.

When you tune into this special place within yourself, you also bring your inner, more perceptive awareness into your physical experiences, where you can see the reflections of your true spiritual nature mirrored in all your everyday activities as you blend your inner knowing into your conscious and subconscious worlds simultaneously.

Your images, intuition, insights, and imagination will teach you the language of your mind and show you your inner knowing. Your true teacher is within. Listen to yourself.

Part Two · *Metaphysical Meditations*

Part Two centers on the theme of self-discovery and spiritual awareness, of exploring the harmony of your body, mind, and spirit, and how they're intricately intertwined. Inside this part, you'll find metaphysical meditations and visualizations to soothe and heal your body, to revitalize and energize you, to open up and expand your mind, and to soar into your spirit.

These meditations share with you the secrets of your soul, if you will listen to the soft, quiet voice that whispers within. They invite you into the center of yourself, to see your spiritual self reflected in all your thoughts and feelings, and in every part of your everyday activities.

These meditations offer you a way to blend your physical consciousness with your spiritual awareness, and to be at one with the world around you and within you. They hold the promise of opening up your inner knowing, as they show you the natural power of your mind and reveal your true spiritual nature, if you will look within yourself to see the images in your imagination— to remember, rediscover, and recognize how special and real they are.

Glorious Gondola

Imagine that you're boarding a beautiful boat, an ornate and glorious gondola, as you begin to travel a magical path—a mystical waterway through your imagination that leads you into your mind and soul—into your spiritual awareness.

The oarsman is a most knowledgeable guide, having traveled this way many times before, who will lead you safely and serenely through all the canals and waterways in this magical, mystical place—your mind.

As you travel your inner journeys through the images, thoughts, and feelings inside you, inside the many multidimensional realms and realities of your soul, and the wonderful worlds of your inner knowing within you, you'll begin to remember and recognize your inherent spiritual symbols.

The world of your inner images—your imagination—shows itself easily through pictures that represent various aspects of your mind and soul.

Some of these symbols are universal, shared by all, but most of them are unique and special to you and are based on your beliefs and frame of reference. The symbols you see may change from time to time, depending on your understanding and interpretation, and on your level of awareness, perception, and insight.

They may also show themselves differently with your current mood, experiences, thoughts, and feelings. Much like your dream images offered to you every night, everything you'll see in your meditations will be very meaningful for you. Be open and receptive to even the smallest details and intricacies, as these hold valuable information and knowledge for you.

In this visualization, the waterway represents your subconscious mind, and the oarsman (guide) is your inner, spiritual self that you may already be aware of or will begin to recognize and remember as you travel the inner journeys in and through your heart, mind, and soul. The boat represents your imagination, the vehicle through which you travel.

Allow your inner self to guide you knowledgeably through all the metaphysical, magical, and mystical paths and places in your mind and heart, through the sometimes hidden and sacred spaces in your soul, and to gently guide you through all the experiences in your life, whether they be inner journeys or outer experiences.

In this self-guided meditation, imagine that you're boarding a boat that can take you anywhere you want to go and for any reason that you want to go there. See what your mind has to show you and what your soul has to share with you. Bon voyage!

Splendor of the Sunset

It's a warm, pleasant evening, and you're out for a quiet stroll, just enjoying the gentle breeze and the subdued, calm feel of the early twilight. As you gaze up toward the horizon and even higher at the sky above you, your attention and awareness is completely caught and absorbed in the sunset.

You see numerous billowy, multicolored clouds etched with layers of radiant mauve combining into varying degrees and shades of orange, ranging from a bright, brilliant orange graduating into tones of peach blending into a pearlish pink that is coalescing and variegating into coral, uniting with hues of rose and highlights of dusky violet mixed with both azure and dusty blue intermingling with nuances of powder gray interspersed on the clouds higher above the horizon, reflecting the beauty and magnificence of the sun's splendor of rays splashed across the twilight sky.

The sky is filled with the most beautiful sunset you've ever seen— the most beautiful sunset in the world. As you experience the awe and wonder, and the majesty and splendor of this ever-changing sunset, you feel the colors within and through every part of you, filling you as you share the sunset with the sky, as you become the sunset, as you breathe in and become one with the essence of the sunset, at one with the essence of twilight that is simultaneously radiant and vibrant, and calm and gentle, with the splendor and subdued energies of the colors illuminating the sky.

The warm, soft breeze gently circles around you, sharing the colors and the quiet feel of early twilight with the earth and the universe as they emanate into and through your spiritual awareness and essence.

As the sun begins to slowly dip and disappear under the horizon, you see the rays of gloriously radiant and vibrant orange and purple hues on the line of the horizon reflected on the bottom of the clouds and mirrored within your mind as they simultaneously ground you to the earth and allow your spirit to soar into the universe.

Breathe in and be the beauty and harmony and splendor of the colors and energies of the sunset inside of you, inside your mind and soul. Feel the vibrations of the colors radiate and expand inside you, flowing outward to the earth and the universe, showing you the many wondrous hues and tones of the colors, and the essence and many expressions of your soul.

Sounds of the Seashore

S it in the warm sand on the beach and enjoy the sights and sounds of the seashore that surround you. Soak up the misty rays of light from the sun that are reflected from the big, puffy, white clouds that float lazily through the azure-blue sky.

Watch the waves as they gently wash upon the shore. Listen to the ebb and flow of the tide. Allow the warmth of the sun and the sound of the waves as they softly splash on the sand to just simply relax you and take you into soothing, serene places within your mind.

Let your thoughts and feelings drift in and out with the sound of the tide. Close your eyes and watch the images inside your mind float gently in tune with the rhythm of the ocean. Feel your mind blending in harmony with the motion of the gentle waves as they softly wash into your awareness.

Breathe in the calm breeze and smell the scent of the ocean air. Be in the pleasant warmth and gentle quiet of this beautiful, perfect day. Just *be*.

Sense yourself—your awareness—blending completely into this soft, soothing, serene moment of here and now, feeling perfectly content and at peace with yourself, at one with the world around you and within you.

Garden of Harmony

Imagine yourself in a very beautiful garden. Looking around, you see many beautiful flowers and lush, flowering bushes spread among open, spacious, grassy areas. The fragrance of the flowers is lovely and pleasing, and the purity of their colors is awe-inspiring.

The bushes and flowers move gently in the soft, warm breeze, creating balance and beauty within the garden and within your mind. The garden emanates a vibrant feeling of energy, radiant and abundant with life and health.

Everything in your garden vibrates in harmony, in tune with nature. It's quiet and peaceful, and the air is clean and pure and refreshing. Breathing in, you sense the oneness of the garden with nature, and you sense that same oneness within yourself as you begin to absorb the harmony and the healing energies of the garden within your body, your mind, and your spirit.

The day is filled with warm sunshine and a brilliant blue sky above you. The light and warmth of the sun on your face and body feels wonderful and rejuvenating. The grass beneath your bare feet feels soft and luxuriant. The healing colors of the blue sky and the green grass surround you, enveloping you with a calm, gentle, soothing, peaceful feeling.

The warmth from the sun's rays begins to permeate and radiate through you, filling you with a wonderful feeling of health and harmony. You feel perfectly in tune with nature and with the universal energies of sunlight.

Within your garden, you feel drawn to a very special place of peace and harmony where you feel most in tune with the healing energies of sunlight and nature all around you. As you enter this special healing place in your garden, you feel completely at peace with yourself and totally in harmony with the beauty and serenity all around you.

In this special healing place, *feel* the vibrations of energy that are both around you and within you. Center in on the warmth and light from the sun. *Feel* the healing energies of sunlight gently vibrating all around you, flowing through you and within you.

Breathe in the sunlight; breathe in the greenness of the earth and the blueness of the sky. Breathe in the health and harmony of this garden deeply inside you—into every part of your body, your mind, and your spirit.

Feel your mind, your thoughts and feelings, and your body vibrating in harmony with the light, totally in tune with both your physical and your spiritual nature, completely in tune with the peaceful, healing energies of your garden. Experience and enjoy the perfect health and harmony you feel within yourself—within your body, your mind, and your spirit.

SUGGESTION

Bring the peace and harmony you feel within every part of you, and the radiant vibrations of light and health you've just experienced, into your conscious mind and let them softly flow through your thoughts and feelings, and your body over and over again.

Allow this Garden of Harmony to become a special place of healing for you whenever you need it, or when you just want to be in a pleasant place to enjoy serenity and peace of mind.

Wonderful Waterfall

It's a pleasantly warm summer day, and you're outside exploring and enjoying the natural wonders and beauties of the earth. You've been hiking for several miles along the base of a softly sloping mountain when you hear the sound of a waterfall. Listening to determine the direction, you let the sound guide you toward the tall bushes and large rocks that you see just beyond the curve ahead of you.

Walking that way, you begin to smell the scent of the water, and you can almost see a rainbow in your mind. Getting closer to the waterfall, the rushing, roaring sound energizes you, and you feel a wonderful power and exhilaration building inside of you.

Parting the bushes, you see a magnificent waterfall gushing with life as it cascades down the mountainside, splashing and shimmering off the rocks and the lush greenery that surrounds it on both sides. Every drop of water sparkles as it catches the sunlight and reflects beautiful rainbows everywhere, pouring into a swirling, foaming pool beneath.

You know that you've discovered a very special place, an area of wonder and beauty, and you laugh with happiness and delight. Stepping through the bushes and getting closer to the waterfall, you feel the misty spray gently touch your face and envelop your body with its magical rainbow aura.

The waterfall is surging with motion. Standing there for a few moments, enjoying the sounds, scents, and sights of this very wonderful place, you watch the waterfall tumbling down the mountainside, sensing its exuberant energy within you.

The pool looks inviting and knowing that it's perfectly safe, you decide to go for a swim, so you drop your backpack and take off your shoes. Stretching in the sunlight and feeling a wonderful sense of aliveness and freedom, you dive into the water, experiencing the coolness and surging motion of the water all around you.

Surfacing, you yell with sheer joy and exuberance, completely in tune with the wonderful, powerful energies of this waterfall. The water refreshes and revitalizes you, invigorating every part of your body, mind, and spirit.

Climbing out of the pool and sitting on the rocks to dry in the warmth of the sun, you feel the powerful energy of the waterfall surging within you, knowing that when you dove into the water, you became part of it and it became part of you.

Crystal Clarity

Closing your eyes and looking inside a special place in your mind, you see a clear crystal ball that radiates with a vibrant energy of light. Looking into the crystal, you sense yourself being drawn into it—beginning to vibrate to the light and energies emanating from the crystal.

The energy seems to come from within the crystal and from within the center of your mind and your essence at the same time. You feel the energies vibrating all around you and within you, radiating out from deep inside you.

As the light and energy vibrations from the crystal—from the light and energies within you—illuminate and energize the imagery of your thoughts and feelings, you feel your mind opening up and expanding, and you begin to see the still and silent images of your thoughts and feelings as they form in your mind and start to sparkle into your awareness.

At first they're blurry and a bit hazy, then they vibrate into a panorama of pictures and a kaleidoscope of images that shape and shift in slow motion through your vision.

Centering your attention and awareness on the images you see within your mind, they become much more sharply focused, more clearly defined and descriptive, and you easily see the pictures of your thoughts and feelings. The pictures are so vivid and detailed that you wonder if you're seeing them with your physical eyes or with your mind's eye.

You open your eyes and look around at the physical things that surround you, and you realize that you're seeing the images of your thoughts and feelings as clearly as you see physical objects. This seems so amazing to you, and so delightful—to see and feel the energy vibrations of your thoughts and feelings with your inner senses.

You close your eyes again and now you notice that the vibrations of the pictures, images, thoughts, and feelings that you see and feel within your mind are transformed into coherent, cohesive, and clear scenes—moving pictures—that you completely understand.

There is a knowing inside you that you've always been able to see and sense the vibrations of your thoughts and feelings as clearly as you see with your physical eyes and experience with your physical senses.

As you realize this, the crystal begins to glow with a radiant, even more luminous, vibration of energy, and you sense your energies and awareness opening up and expanding even more within your mind.

The crystal has become a glowing ball of energy, emanating a vibrant radiance and a brilliant light that gently enters in and through every part of your mind as the inner vibrations of your thoughts and feelings open up in much more detail and clarity inside you, becoming much more energized within you.

It's an incredible, wonderful, magical feeling. You know that you have the power to clearly and consciously see and sense and feel and understand both the seen and unseen energy vibrations that emanate from all your thoughts and feelings.

But even more than that, you're able to see into and through anything and everything—into all the emotions and events and experiences in your life, to understand and know every part of them, and to see the expressions of your thoughts and feelings from the inside out.

The energy vibrations and the light from within the crystal—the energy vibrations within you, within your mind—are becoming stronger and more clearly defined, completely opening up inside of you and expanding into multidimensional realms of insight, knowing, and awareness.

NOTES

There are some very special fringe benefits to this meditation that you may have just discovered, and will definitely discover the more you work with it to strengthen your innate powers of inner seeing and sensing (insight and intuition).

In addition to helping you learn how to visualize—to see with your mind's eye—and to intuitively sense, through your inner perceptions, by illuminating the imagery of your thoughts and feelings, this meditation also shows you how you energize and express your thoughts and feelings in and through all your experiences—how they first become real in your mind and then manifest in your life, showing you how you create your own reality.

This meditation also helps you to clearly see and understand the symbols and imagery in both your dreams and your everyday experiences and to accurately interpret them.

As is true with all the meditations in this book, you'll discover more than what is apparent on the surface and just below it—you'll travel deeper and further than that. There's much more to experience and know. Explore and enjoy.

Releasing a Request

You have a very special request, a hope you'd like to see realized, or a dream you'd like to have come true, or a question you'd like to have answered, or perhaps a problem you'd like to have solved.

Think about your request very carefully and in great detail. Ponder all the reasons why you want it and how you'll feel when it is granted. See what you will do with it when you receive it, and how you will share it.

Imagine all the things that may need to occur in your life before your request is granted. See those things happening in your mind and be open to receiving other ideas, insights, and images that show you things you may not have thought of or considered yet.

Feel a wonderful sense of hope in your heart, and believe that your request is manifesting even as you think about it. Be loving in your desire and appreciative in your anticipation. Simply feel the joy of it in your soul.

Begin to put your thoughts, feelings, insights, ideas, and images into motion by taking action on them to bring them into being. Be spontaneous and free with your actions, going with the flow of them, listening to your inner thoughts and following your feelings.

Trust and know that your request will come to be, yet remain detached from achieving specific results so that even better things can occur.

As you prepare to receive the fulfillment of your request, you may decide to also ask for help from higher sources so that whatever happens will be the most beneficial for everyone who is involved or who will be touched by it.

In your mind, write your request on a piece of paper, pouring out all your thoughts and feelings about it. Then give the paper to a beautiful white dove who is waiting on the sill of an open window.

As the dove flies into the universe with your request, you know that it is being fulfilled in the proper timing and in the most appropriate manner for the highest good of all.

Hidden Horizons

Walking along the beach, you gaze out to the horizon, wondering what is beyond your line of vision. You think you'd like to go exploring to discover what's really out there—what's beyond your conscious knowing—but you think it's impossible to swim that far.

But what if you could? What if there were a way? It's just a thought, a muse in your mind, but you entertain the idea, curious to know. You put your toes in the water; it's warm and welcoming.

As you continue to walk along the beach by the edge of the shore, splashing in the water and looking for seashells, you happen upon a small but sturdy boat. This offers you some wonderful choices and an exciting opportunity.

You can decide to stay by the seashore and wonder what the horizon holds. You're having a very pleasant experience here, and you may want to just enjoy it more completely, to think about what might be beyond the horizon and to ponder the possibilities.

You can decide to go for a short sail, drifting through the waves close to shore, seeing things you're familiar and comfortable with, becoming more aware of them, and enjoying the rhythm and motion of the water and the waves.

You can decide to be swept out to sea, gently flowing and floating in this safe, secure boat that can take you into uncharted waters, perhaps into other realms and realities of perception and awareness where you can see and explore a bigger, broader perspective, and where you can expand your consciousness to experience things that you may have never seen before or perhaps have just never noticed, or to experience them in a different way.

You can experience this meditation in several ways. You can use it as a visualization to gain more information to help you understand the challenges and choices you're facing in your physical reality, to give yourself some distance from them so you can clearly tune into your true thoughts and feelings, and to get a better look at the overall picture of your experiences.

If you're ready to take risks or are thinking about making some changes in your life, you can sail away to see [sea] their possible and probable outcomes before they're played out in your reality, and to change things that have not yet occurred. When you return to shore [sure], you may discover that things are very different than they first appeared to be.

If you feel adventuresome and are daring enough, you can use this visualization to help encourage and self-empower you on your inner journeying, on your path of self-discovery and spiritual awareness. You decide where you want to go and how far you want to travel into and perhaps beyond the hidden horizons of your mind.

Or you can just simply set sail and see what happens. This meditation works for a little leap of faith or a giant lunge of trust. You can explore the boundaries beyond your conscious reality, beyond the physical structure of time and space into the multidimensionality of your soul. Whatever way you choose to travel and wherever your journey takes you, it can prove to be very interesting and enlightening.

Canvas of Creation

You're in an artist's studio where there are many colors of paint, and lots of brushes and blank canvasses—tools for you to create all the experiences you'd like to have in your life. Ideas begin to sparkle inside your imagination as you think about what you'd like to create.

You know that this is a special studio and that you can come here whenever you want to paint more pictures. Perhaps your studio is open and airy. Perhaps it has a skylight and sliding glass doors around every side that open into a beautiful nature scene, maybe a garden or a meadow or a magical forest.

Perhaps it's a large, spacious loft with lots of room for all the many pictures—the masterpieces—that you know you'll paint here. Maybe your artist's studio is a frame of mind, a magical place of insight, inspiration, thought, and wonder in your creative awareness. Or perhaps it's somewhere in the universe, a special place that is illuminated with a mystical light.

Looking inside your imagination—inside your thoughts and feelings—you feel magically inspired as you begin to paint some of the pictures you'd like to experience in your life, filling in details with descriptive images and flashes of insight.

Delighted, you discover that you have a real flair and talent for this. As you allow the artist in you to emerge and come forth, you feel a wonderful power building within you as you realize that you can create whatever you want, and that you hold within your hands all the creative tools you need to sketch and draw, and shape and sculpt the many images and expressions of your experiences.

Pausing for a moment, you stand back to admire your work. Looking at your partially-completed pictures to study what you've just created and to decide how to enhance them and what finishing touches and flourishes you'd like to add, you notice that somehow, magically, the canvasses have begun to come to life and to become the experiences you painted.

They're three-dimensional as they move and become alive in your experiences. They're living, breathing, being and becoming images and expressions of your thoughts, and feelings that created them. You see both the illusionary and the tangible nature of your thoughts, and how they become real first in your mind and then in the manifest world.

The pictures, and the tones and hues of the colors, are ever-changing in every moment, influenced by your choices, and by every nuance of your thoughts and feelings; every action and reaction you have changes and thereby affects and alters your original ideas, insights, and experiences, creating new and various expressions to the work of art that is your life in motion

Cushiony Clouds

You're outside on a beautiful, warm, sunny day, lying in a softly-swaying hammock, just enjoying the gentle breeze and the sunshine. Looking up at the sky, you see a few puffy white clouds floating leisurely by, and you notice how blue and expansive the sky is.

You wonder what it would be like to float through the sky on a puffy white cloud. Would it be the same as swinging in your hammock or would it be completely different?

You decide to find out for yourself. Using your imagination, you project yourself into the sky, onto that puffy white cloud. Feeling free and light, weightless, unrestrained by gravity, you're floating along, carefree and happy. The cloud supports you with a cushiony softness that is unlike anything you've ever experienced.

As the cloud floats along, directed by unseen universal winds, you begin to wonder where it's going, but this thought doesn't really concern you. You're quite content to just go with the flow, to be completely here now in the present moment, to experience the calm, relaxing feeling of simply floating on the gentle breeze.

Every once in a while, you peer over the side of the cloud and look down at the earth, knowing you can return at any time and that you're perfectly safe where you are.

Even though the cloud seems to be drifting in the wind, you know that there's a universal direction it follows, a natural flow of energy, and that this cloud has its own purpose for being.

You wonder what that purpose might be, and you merge your consciousness with the cloud's consciousness to discover its reason for existence. Surprisingly, the cloud has a lot to say. Seemingly floating aimlessly along, it has seen and experienced many wonderful and magical things.

It has traveled the world in many forms: sometimes as the puffy white cloud it is now, floating softly on a gentle breeze; sometimes disappearing and dissipating in the light of the sun, reappearing when it draws moisture from the earth, being nourished from its physical source.

Sometimes it appears as a dark, black cloud, rolling and roaring through the sky as it thunders and creates lightning, invigorating and energizing the earth; sometimes pouring rain, and other times giving a gentle shower of rain, sharing nourishment with the earth.

You become aware that even though at times it may seem that your life appears to be like this puffy white cloud as it is expressing itself at this moment, seemingly drifting aimlessly along, that there is a unique and very special purpose that you have in life and that perhaps you're just floating along for the moment, either relaxing or gathering information and energy that will manifest in another form for a particular purpose.

Perfectly content to travel gently on this puffy white cloud in the sky, you continue to float along, thinking your thoughts and knowing that everything you do and experience is part of a perfect plan you've created for yourself, and that all the events in your life have a very special purpose and meaning, and a reason for existence.

There are many other things that this cloud can tell you and share with you, and many special, magical things that it can show and offer you. You smile to yourself, thinking that this cloud is your magic carpet ride to anywhere you want to go and is also a mentor for your thoughts.

Just like the cloud, you're going with the flow, sometimes merging with other clouds, sometimes floating free and alone, just enjoying the journey of being here now, in the present moment. You think about how wonderful and free this cloud is, about how wonderful and free you are.

Suddenly you're back in your hammock, swaying softly in the gentle breeze, looking up at the puffy white clouds in the sky, knowing the mysteries of your mind and how powerful and truly awesome your awareness is.

You smile to yourself, knowing that you've discovered something very wonderful and magical. You've discovered that your consciousness exists separately from your physical body, and that your thoughts are free to travel on the energy of air inside what appears to be a cushiony white mist of illusion in the sky.

Verdant Valley

You're standing at the rim of a gently sloping valley. Looking into the valley, you see how green and healthy and beautiful everything is. The sun radiates sparkles of light from a softly-winding stream of water in the center. The gentle breeze and warmth of the day invite you for a walk.

Noticing a footpath that leads down through the lush, flowering bushes into the verdant valley below, you decide to follow the path to see where it leads. As you walk, admiring and appreciating the beauty and tranquillity all around you, you sense this same feeling of peace within you, and you know that you've found the path that leads you within to your spiritual self.

You're now in the center of the valley by the sparkling stream of water. Everything is lush and green and beautiful. There are a few trees by the water, and a forest rests quietly beyond the open space behind you. You see a mountain in the distance to your right, rising up majestically into the horizon, into the sky.

Standing here for a few moments to just simply enjoy being in this beautiful, peaceful place in nature, you listen to the gentle sounds of nature all around you—to the flow of the water over the small pebbles in the brook, hearing the song it sings to you and the unspoken words in your soul, and hearing and feeling the soft sound of the wind as it whispers quietly through the leaves of the trees beside you, creating a blissful, beautiful harmony, as the sounds of nature speak softly to your heart, mind, and soul.

You feel so completely natural and comfortable here, tranquil and at home, totally in tune with nature, and centered within yourself.

Joyfully you stretch your arms wide in an open embrace of all that is around you, turning once in a circular motion to encompass all of nature, then bringing your arms in toward your chest, hugging and gently holding nature close to your heart.

Closing your eyes for a moment, you deeply breathe in the pure, clean air, completely experiencing and sensing nature all around you, bringing it deeply within yourself—being fully in and reconnecting with nature, with every part of you—feeling the joy, peace, and harmony. Opening your eyes, you smile at the wonder-filled world around you and within you.

Taking your shoes off, you feel the soft, luxuriant grass beneath your bare feet, as the earth shares its soft, nurturing essence with you. You feel the gentle, caressing energy of the earth vibrating quietly and softly.

Noticing that the water is ankle deep, you step into it, feeling it softly move around your feet and through your toes. The water is cool and refreshing; it feels wonderful on your skin as it gently surges and swirls around your feet.

Standing in this sparkling, gently swirling stream of water, you feel rejuvenated and sense the energy of your spiritual nature rising up within you, becoming open and expansive and free.

Laughing with happiness, you squat down closer to the water, listening to it gently ripple and flow over and around the pebbles you can clearly see beneath the surface.

Joyfully splashing the water all around you with your hands, you feel that same surge of gentle energy vibrate through your hands, and you notice how the drops of water catch the sunlight and radiate rainbows.

Slowly and thoughtfully, you stand up and walk through the water to a quiet pool that you see a few steps away.

You look up into the azure-blue sky, seeing the soft wisps of a few billowy white clouds floating leisurely above you, and you feel the warmth of the sun gently caressing your face and skin.

Looking down at the still, calm pool of water, you notice how the sunshine sparkles and shimmers on the water, reflecting the blueness of the sky and the white wispiness of the clouds.

Looking into the clear, sparkling water, you see the pebbles beneath the surface. A gentle breeze ripples the water, softly caressing it.

Stepping out of the water and kneeling down to look into the pool, you see more than the reflection of your physical self. Shimmering in the water is the essence of your inner, spiritual self, moving around and through your image in gentle ripples.

You notice how the water reflects and mirrors the sunlight and the sky above you, and you recognize that your physical self is really a mirror of your spiritual self.

At the same time, you realize that the reality of your everyday world goes much deeper than your conscious mind, much farther than the physical realm you live in. Below the surface of every thought and feeling and all around you in every experience, your spiritual self waits ever so quietly to be recognized, to be heard.

Sitting beside the sparkling stream of water in this beautiful, vibrantly verdant valley, you begin to listen quietly to your thoughts, to your inner voice, just as you earlier listened to the quiet sounds of nature, feeling and hearing them all around you and within you at the same time.

You feel completely at home here, centered in your heart and mind, and connected with your essence, in tune with your true nature.

You know that the voice you hear in your mind is your spiritual self whispering softly to you in your thoughts and feelings, and through your dreams and experiences. As you listen, you know you can feel and be completely aware of all the many expressions and ripples of your experiences as you travel through them, joyfully following the path that leads you within.

Key to Knowledge

You're somewhere in the universe in a huge hallway with arched ceilings. A radiant light emanates from everywhere around you, illuminating the doorways that line the hall, extending farther than the eye can see. Wondering what is inside each room, you try to open the first door on your right but discover to your dismay that it's locked.

Undaunted and more curious now to know what is inside, you pause to think as you contemplate this dilemma for a moment. Considering where you are and why you're here, and what you've been looking for in your life, you intuitively know that the doors open into all the magical, wonderful worlds within yourself, into your inner knowing and your spiritual awareness, and that within each room are the secrets to your soul and the answers to all the mysteries of the universe.

Determined to find a way inside and wishing that you had a key, you feel a warm tingle in your hand—a vibration of energy—and you hear a popping sound. In a flashing sparkle of light, an ornate golden key appears in your hand.

This seems so miraculous to you—that the key magically appeared out of nowhere the moment you wished for it. Turning it over in your hand and feeling its warmth and energy, then cupping it in the palm of your hand, caressing it with the fingers of your other hand, you know that this is a most wondrous and powerful key because it opens the doors to all the magic and knowledge inside your mind and offers you the treasures of truth. At the same time, you know that you've always held within you the key that could open up your mind and your spiritual awareness.

You insert the key into the lock and stand there for a moment, enjoying the wonderful feeling of happy anticipation and joy within you, knowing that you're about to begin a very wonderful journey. Turning the key, you open the door easily.

Crossing the threshold, you enter the room with a feeling of respect and awe, knowing that you have gained access to universal wisdom and knowledge, and that you're now able to discover and explore all the wonders of the many worlds within you, to discover everything you've always wanted to know and more.

You know that you've given yourself a special, magical, wonderful gift—that you hold the key to knowledge in your hand—a key that gives you entry into your inner, spiritual self and opens the doors into all your knowledge, into the multidimensional worlds of the universe both within you and all around you.

Special Sanctuary

Remember a treasured, private place you enjoyed and explored as a child—a special, secret space that no one else knew about—a place you could go when you wanted to be alone. Perhaps it was a real place, or perhaps it only seemed to exist in your imagination.

It's the place where you enjoyed being peaceful, safe, and happy within yourself. A special sanctuary where you felt completely comfortable and natural, where you could truly be who you really are. A magical place where you could open up your true feelings and listen to yourself. A place where you could be with your inner child or your imaginary friend.

It's the place where you can again connect with your true spiritual nature, where you can nourish your soul and experience total harmony within yourself. It's the place that waits for you to remember it and to visit it again.

It's probably the same place you go to now (although it may appear different than it did when you were a child) when you want to be alone with your thoughts and feelings, and when you need to reconnect with the inner, vital part of you—your inner self.

This meditation is a self-guided visualization into a private, spiritual place within you. Simply close your eyes and see, imagine, remember, and re-create your special sanctuary in your mind. Go inside the world of your inner images and be inside your safe, special sanctuary again.

As you reexplore it, see how it's different and how it has remained the same. Spend some time there to become familiar with it again, and to enjoy and appreciate it.

Tune into your feelings, open up your insights and impressions. Really notice how you feel when you're there; notice the atmosphere and the ambiance. Notice what you do and what you think about when you first enter your special sanctuary after being away from it for so long.

You may be pleasantly surprised to find your imaginary friend or your inner child waiting for you, and you may also discover that your imaginary friend or your inner child is all grown up now, too, just as you are. Embrace and reunite with yourself.

Little Lost Leaf

You're outside for a walk, going nowhere in particular, just walking for exercise and enjoyment, and to get your thoughts clear on changes you're making in your life. Perhaps you feel a bit disconnected, as if you've outgrown something and you're searching for a new sense of direction, a new way to grow. It's a beautiful autumn day, and the changing leaves on the trees are very colorful and vibrant.

You notice a little leaf that has fallen to the ground. It calls to you, asking to be noticed, wanting to share its essence with you. It's a very beautiful and unusual, very unique and individual, multicolored leaf, orange and red and yellow.

Picking it up, perhaps feeling a bit sad at first that it has lost its connection to the tree, you soon begin to realize that it is following its course of direction and purpose, beginning a new journey that ultimately leads to renewal and growth.

You compare this leaf to yourself and to the changing seasons, to the changes in life. Perhaps you are going through changes in your life, perhaps feeling a little sad and lost yourself as you make changes, let go of connections, and prepare for new directions in your life. Perhaps you've outgrown something, and it is time to move on, to explore new options and choices.

Perhaps you're unsure of your direction. You look at the leaf and notice that it is ready to move forward in its life cycle—saying good-bye, letting go with love. You admire its courage, knowing that you must find that same courage within yourself to move on.

You relate to this leaf and feel a deep, inner sense of kinship and familiarity with it. Like you, the leaf has outgrown this particular connection. You look at the tree that it has fallen from and feel a sincere gratefulness and appreciation for the growth that this leaf has experienced, for the growth that you've experienced, for the connection that enabled you to grow and flourish and now to move on to a new direction in your life—a new course of exploration and growth.

You begin to explore your inner essence, going within yourself to see the changes you're contemplating in your life, and to renew and revitalize yourself, making ready to burst forth anew in the spring, allowing the budding and blossoming of your soul to renew itself from deep within.

Spirit of the Wind

Feel yourself surrounded by a magical wind. It does not flow in any one direction; it spirals in a light, breezy dance all around you. It encircles you from your feet up and from your head down, carrying you way up into the sky, into the universe, and bringing you gently down to the earth again.

Breathe in this magical wind and notice its sweet perfume, its wonderful fragrance and aroma. It smells like the richness of the earth—wet grass, lilacs, roses, and many other beautiful scents commingling together.

As you breathe in this magical wind, it cleanses and purifies you, clearing all the cobwebs from the corners of your mind, refreshing your spirit, filling you with peace and harmony. As you breathe out this magical wind and merge your breath, your being, with its essence, you feel your spirit becoming intertwined with the spirit of the wind. As you continue breathing and being with the wind, you feel it expanding in all directions around you.

The wind makes you feel totally light, as if you are weightless. You are part of it, you are connected with the spirit of this magical wind. You have become at one with the spirit of the wind. It lifts you up into the sky and supports you on a current of air.

As you look down at the earth, you see it stretching for miles beneath you. You see its rivers, its hills, its cities, its open fields and meadows, its forests and its gardens.

Feel the spirit of the wind gently breathing out of you, lightly blessing the earth, touching and caressing everything that is there, as light as a song and as free as a dance. Sing and dance with the wind.

Special Spring Morning

It's a wonder-filled, beautiful day, a time in the spring when the world is waking up from a winter's sleep. As the sunshine pours in through an open window, you breathe in the fresh, clean scent of the air—the wonderful smell of an early spring morning—and enjoy the feeling of being alive on such a beautiful day.

You go outside to completely enjoy and experience this beautiful day, with its promise of renewal and growth, its vibrancy and essence. You notice the greenness all around you and the tender buds and blossoms on the trees and bushes as they begin to open up and welcome their new beginnings, to embrace their reawakening.

Feeling the gentle warmth of the sun on your face and skin, and the breeze as it caresses you softly, you listen to the harmonious sounds you hear, the sound of birds chirping and the breeze singing through the leaves on the trees. You hear the sunshine sparkling all around you. But even more than that, you hear the sounds of nature coming alive.

Looking at the sparkling dewdrops on the lush, green grass and on the tips of the leaves on the bushes, you notice the delicate rainbows sparkling with life, radiating multicolored auras that touch them softly, caressingly, and playing with the sunshine emanating and radiating from them. It's almost as if the rainbows are alive, expressing their joy at the beauty and renewal of life, and feeling blessed to be part of this beautiful day.

Looking at the early spring flowers in bloom, at their intricacy and detail, and the delicate profusion and variety of buds on the trees and bushes, you touch them gently and lovingly, feeling their texture and smelling their wonderful fragrance and aroma.

You see every detail of them, noticing the hues and tones of color, each nuance and form. You see how they're beginning to open up, and you feel that same sense of your essence opening up within you, showing all the beauty you have inside you and expressing the joy of your soul on this beautiful, magical spring morning.

You know that your spirit is coming alive again, and you know that you're part of all the things you feel and see and sense and hear and know and experience as you enjoy all the scents and sounds of a beautiful spring morning with every part of you.

But most of all, you notice and are completely aware of your spiritual renewal and rejuvenation on this beautiful day. You notice your spiritual reawakening and your affinity with the world of nature as it is nourished and nurtured from the light of the sun and from the light within you.

Harmony of Home

You're inside the presence of a wonderful warmth and light that feels completely nurturing, safe, and peaceful, a light that brings you feelings of love, joy, and harmony.

Inside this presence are the most beautiful colors that you can imagine, colors that go beyond what words can fully describe. Perhaps you see the colors as a rainbow shimmering in the sky or as a scenic panorama of pictures blending into one another.

You feel this light as having the texture or sensation of something very soft, smooth, and silky, like the fur of a beloved pet, a cat or a dog that snuggles up to you for love, warmth, and safety, totally trusting you, seeking and giving companionship and unconditional love.

Breathing in the wonderful aroma of this presence—perhaps it smells like lilacs or the wetness of the earth just after it has rained, or maybe the scent is that of an early spring morning, bursting forth, blossoming and blooming with buds and vibrantly green growth—it offers you the promise of a new beginning and shares with you an eternal essence of life.

Tasting the essence of this presence—maybe it is like your favorite cookies, just baked, warm and gooey-soft from the oven, melting in your mouth, or of fresh, clear water quenching your thirst and refreshing you—it nurtures you with a wonderful feeling and sense of security and safety.

Listening to the presence as it softly moves into and through your spirit like a gentle breeze blowing through your soul, it fills your mind and your emotions with harmony and peace, in tune with your true nature, playing a symphony that sounds like beautiful wind chimes, a celestial song of joy and love.

You feel completely at home with, connected to, and at one with all aspects of this presence; it permeates your entire being, healing and harmonizing every part of your body, mind, and spirit. As this gentle, loving energy flows through you, you know that this presence is you; this presence is your soul.

Feel yourself completely enveloped with the warmth and the light that is both around you and within you. Experience and enjoy all the sights, scents, feelings, tastes, and sounds, as your soul embraces you with the harmony of home and reawakens you to your true spiritual nature.

Vision Quest

You begin to follow a path that leads you into a tropical rain forest that is lush and green. Beams and shafts of light filter through the thick canopy of leaves that open up to the sky in bright-blue splashes and glimpses of pure-white clouds. You feel completely safe and comfortable as you walk forward on your vision quest.

Perhaps you clearly know what you are seeking or you know that you'll recognize it when you see it, or perhaps your vision quest is totally open to whatever you experience on this journey of your soul for knowledge. Totally trusting and knowing that you will find what you are truly searching for, you continue to go deeper within.

Clouds begin to gather, and you hear the distant rumble of thunder and see occasional bright flashes of lightning, and you smell the scent of rain in the air. It is becoming darker as the rain approaches, but you feel safe guided by your soul. You feel intimately connected with this forest, this place of sacredness that you have entered.

You notice beautiful bushes all around you that are filled with blooms of many kinds of flowers you've never seen before and with delicate orchids and multicolored wildflowers. Their colors are vibrant, and the flowers emanate a wonderful fragrance.

Closing your eyes for a moment and breathing in, you completely sense and absorb the colors and the fragrances within you and—in a way that you somehow completely understand—you become the colors, you become the flowers, you become the fragrance, you become one with their essence.

As the rain begins to drop softly, you hear the gentle patter on the leaves. Opening your eyes, you see the water dripping from the tips of the leaves and smell the rich scent of the wet earth as you feel the moisture in the air all around you.

Again, you close your eyes for a moment and completely experience and absorb the feel of the rain on your skin and the warm, gentle breeze, and the sound of the raindrops on the leaves. You become one with the essence of the rain, the scent of the earth, the feel of the air, and with the leaves as they are touched and nourished by the rain.

As suddenly as it began, the rain stops and the sun bursts forth, sparkling with light and radiating dazzling rainbows on the water dripping from the leaves. Even with your eyes closed, you see the vibrancy and feel the energy and aura of the forest.

Opening your eyes and looking all around, you know that you're experiencing the essence of life, the sharing of the earth with the universe, seeing how the universe nourishes the earth, birthing and bringing forth new life, and nurturing the life that is already growing. You begin to become aware of how your soul—your spirit—shares with you and nourishes you.

Continuing on your vision quest, walking upon the path through the rain forest—the path that leads you within to your soul, to your essence—you come to a tall tree with a door in its trunk, an open door that beckons you within. Knowing that you're completely safe, you enter.

Although you expected it to be dark, you see that it is lit with a radiant light from within that glows everywhere, illuminating everything it touches. This light has a special feeling and quality to it, an ambiance and essence that is both tangible and intangible at the same time, that emanates and opens up feelings that are at once familiar and foreign to you. Then you begin to remember, to know all that is within you.

You see a magical, mystical world opening up and unfolding before you. Gazing joyfully all around you, you know that you've found what your soul was searching for and that your vision quest has shown you the way to a special place inside your soul, a sacred space that offers you many treasures and gifts of insight and wisdom, a spiritual place that is your sanctuary, and within this sanctuary you become aware of many things your soul has always known.

Perhaps there is a guide who has been waiting for you who now comes forward to greet you, to walk with you through this wonderful world, and to show and share with you many experiences that your soul desires to have. Perhaps you recognize this guide as a spiritual friend you've traveled with before, or perhaps this guide is a new friend who has a special connection with you.

Or perhaps somewhere, deep inside you, you have a knowingness that this guide is your higher self, who has been waiting, ever so patiently and lovingly, for you to become aware of the true essence of yourself— your soul—and to remember all the spiritual knowledge you have within you.

Explore and experience every part of this sacred place within yourself and allow your guide to take you wherever you want to go, to be both your companion and your way-shower as you find everything that you're looking for on your vision quest that leads you into your soul.

Being at the Beach

It's a warm, sunny day, and you're at the beach. Listen to the splash of the waves and the sound of the water as it comes to the shore. As you walk along the beach, feel the softness and warmth of the sand beneath your feet. Perhaps you notice a few seashells that have been washed ashore by the tide, and you pick them up to admire them.

As you continue walking along the beach, you find a small, secluded cove next to some large rocks that stretch across the sand. It's quiet and private, and it's a perfect place to lie on your beach towel. As you get comfortable on your towel, you feel the sand adjust to your body. As you lie on the beach, you begin to feel the warmth of the sun on your skin as it gently permeates your body.

The sky is an azure-blue, with a few puffy white clouds floating leisurely by. The sun is bright and strong, and feels pleasantly warm on your body. You feel a gentle breeze and smell the scent of your suntan lotion. You hear the sound of seagulls and the muted talk and laughter of other people in the distance. You feel so relaxed and peaceful; the quiet hum of conversation sounds like soft, gentle music.

As you lie on the beach, you listen to the water as it comes to the shore and as it returns to the ocean. As the tide ebbs and flows, your breathing begins to match the rhythm of the tide—in and out, back and forth. The sound of the ocean is lulling, soothing, and relaxing. The sounds ebb and flow, forming a gentle, rhythmic pattern that moves in tune with your thoughts and feelings.

The sun is pleasantly warm on your body, and the sound of the ocean completely relaxes you. All your thoughts flow into a gentle awareness of this beautiful day. You feel a wonderful contentment and peace. You're enjoying the warmth of the sun and the rhythm of the tide; you're in harmony with everything you're experiencing.

Majestic Mountain

Picture a gently sloping valley with a softly winding stream of water in the center. The sun radiates sparkles of light from the water, and everything is lush and green and beautiful. There are a few trees by the water, and a forest rests quietly beyond the open space behind you. You've been here before, you recognize the stream of water that you enjoyed earlier in the Verdant Valley and now you think you'd like to explore more of what it has to offer.

Looking upward, you see a mountain in the distance to your right, rising majestically above the horizon into the soft, misty white clouds in the sky. Even though the top of the mountain seems to be hidden within the clouds, you can somehow magically see through the soft, white mist into the universe, and you know within your mind that you can travel up to the top of the mountain and beyond.

Thinking this thought, you find yourself at the top of this majestic mountain, peering down through the misty clouds at the earth below you, seeing through the illusions that had previously clouded your spiritual vision—your insight and inner knowing.

Returning your gaze upward, elevating your awareness and opening up your inner knowing and spiritual insight, you see above the clouds that momentarily seemed to obscure your vision as you simultaneously look within yourself.

As you pierce the veil of awareness that had previously cloaked your soul with the illusions of your physical experiences, you completely open up your mind as your spirit rises into the majesty of your soul above the mountain.

Part Three — *Magical Meditations*

Part Three centers on the theme of remembering and reopening your inner knowing and the world you experienced as a child. It shows your interrelationship and harmony with the earth and the universe. Inside this part, you'll find magical meditations and visualizations to make your heart happy, to make your mind more aware, and to make your soul sing.

These meditations share with you a way to rediscover and reawaken all the magic you experienced then and can enjoy again now. They invite you to reach within, to embrace your inner child, and to tune into your inner self—to stretch above and beyond yourself into your soul— to remember the knowledge of the universe, the secrets of nature and the earth, and to share your essence and harmony with the earth and the universe as you reconnect with yourself.

These meditations offer you a way to bring the physical and spiritual worlds together and blend them into your everyday world, into every experience in your life. They hold the promise of reunions with the spiritual side of yourself, if you will look within your heart, mind, and soul to remember, rediscover, and recognize the magic that exists within you.

Magical Melodies

You enter a quiet, warmly lit room that appears to be empty, yet you sense—you know—that there is a wonderful treasure here, a very special, spiritual gift that drew you to this subdued, magical room.

Looking around, you notice a small, delicately decorated music box. Opening it, you hear a beautiful melody begin to play. The sounds are harmonious and gentle, soft and soothing, bringing you into a peaceful place within yourself.

Delighted, you close your eyes to more fully experience and appreciate the music as it richly fills every part of the acoustically perfect room—as it fills all your senses with pure enjoyment and reverberates softly into and through your body, heart, and mind.

Listen to the music inside your mind as it lightly resonates into your thoughts and feelings, plays gently through your heart, and softly sings into your soul.

As you completely tune yourself in to the harmony of the tones and the sounds of the feelings that the music inspires and brings forth within you, you feel yourself—your awareness—expanding, ever so gently into your spiritual essence.

The music becomes part of you, and you know that the music you hear comes from a place of memory deep within you.

It's the celestial music of the universe—the symphony of your soul. The song sings to you of home, calling to you softly and gently. This magical, mystical music box plays a melody of harmony, peace, and love within you—the natural vibration of your soul.

Listening to the melody, you remember and know that you can hear a seed when it springs forth from the earth, gently birthing and bringing new life. You can hear a flower as it buds and blooms and sings in the sunshine.

You can hear a rock whisper to you from deep within the earth. You know the voice of the wind as it silently blows through the leaves of a tree, and you understand the symphony of the stars as they share the secrets of the universe.

Flowing River

You are on a boat floating down a gently flowing river. The water is clear and is the most beautiful shade of blue-green that you have ever seen. On both sides of the river are a colorful profusion of flowers, shrubs, and trees of many varieties.

You notice that your boat is very special and sturdy. It is made of different kinds of wood from all over the world. You notice the peaceful motion of the boat and how it floats gently upon the water, moving smoothly and effortlessly through the water and streams of life.

The river opens into a great sea. There are many other boats sailing upon this ocean. Together, they sail into the wide-open sea. You are all going on a glorious journey to fulfill a spiritual mission.

As you travel together, all of you are helping to bring to the world the experience of the awakening of every soul to its divine nature.

See where your boat leads you. Explore where it takes you. Know what your part and purpose is in this divine reawakening of every soul's awareness.

As you journey where your boat takes you, you become fully awake and aware of your mission of being a way-shower, of illuminating the path that will help to guide other souls into their light.

And you remember that at the time you most needed to be shown the way to your path, a way-shower was there for you, showing you the way and guiding you.

As the ocean returns you to the gently flowing river, you notice the lighthouse that shines its beacon of light brightly over the water, the stream of life.

As you go toward the light, you appreciate your magical journey through life as you sail your boat to the harbor you call home.

Wonderful Wishes

Gazing at the clear twilight sky, you see the first star sparkling brightly in the universe. As a child, you knew that wishes were filled with magic, and you remember wishing upon a star, believing that whatever you wished for would come true.

The star invites your attention and asks for your wish. There is a special hope and feeling inside you that whatever you wish will be granted.

Looking inside your mind—your heart—you think about all the wonderful things you'd like and what you would do if you had them.

Focusing on your most desired and treasured wish, you look up at the brightly twinkling star, and you know, in a special *knowing* place inside you, that your wish will come true, if only you believe it to be so in your heart and your mind.

As you make your wish on this beautiful star in the universe, it becomes a falling star, shooting gracefully and majestically to the earth, and you know that magically, your wish is already on its way to becoming true, to being real in your physical world.

Spiritual Sun Ray

You're in a circular clearing in a magical forest. It's still and quiet, and you feel very peaceful and spiritual here. You sense a mystical aura and ambiance in this special, sacred place within the forest that brings forth feelings of reverence inside you. You feel as if you're somewhere inside your soul rather than in a forest.

A gentle breeze caresses you and seems to touch you somewhere inside yourself. The trees all around you softly whisper through the wind to you, as if they have something of great importance to tell you—a spiritual secret. Listening to the whispers and looking around, you notice golden beams of sunlight shining through the leaves of the trees.

Standing in the center of the clearing, you look up to the sky and notice how the beams of light become brighter, sparkling and shimmering above the tops of the trees as they create intricate and interwoven patterns on the forest floor that are ever-changing in the gentle breeze. It's as if the gentle touch of the wind and the light from the sun combine their essence to create the mystical ambiance all around you.

You can both see and sense that the wind and the light are freer and clearer above the forest. At first you think it's because there is nothing to block the flow of air or to filter the light, and, while this is true, you realize at the same time that there is more to it than that. You recognize the similarity between what the universe is showing you and what you experience in your life when you go within yourself, when you look within your mind.

You see that this is also true of your spiritual awareness, and that when you go above the various influences and interferences of your day-to-day activities and the physical energies of your experiences, everything is clearer and brighter, and your awareness is purer, not filtered in any way.

But there is something even more special than this insight that the wind and the light have to share with you now.

The light looks warm and welcoming; it beckons to you and invites you within. As you step into a beam of light, it becomes brighter, and you feel energized and empowered. You have a sense, a knowing within you, that this light is part of you and that there is a special quality that you share with the light.

As the wind whispers into your mind and the ray of sunlight energizes your spirit, you somehow know, in a sacred place inside your soul, that you can travel this magical sun ray into the center of the sun.

A vague memory begins to open up within you that you've done this before. As a child, you would often play with the rays of light from the sun and travel the first rays of the sunrise to dance with other spirits of the dawn. You also remember that there is a special treasure in the center of the sun, though you can't remember exactly what it is right now.

As you're standing in this beam of light, feeling its energy and power, you look at all the golden sun rays that surround you, and the memory begins to become more clear in your mind. You know that the treasure is the light of your soul that opens up your spiritual knowledge and that this gift is one given to all souls and is meant for sharing.

You know that all you have to do to receive and open this gift is to know that it is already yours; it is your spiritual birthright. Looking upward, you begin to travel through the light of the sun ray into the sun, flying and soaring high above the earth into the universe, into the center of the sun.

As the spirit of the sun gives you your special gift—the light of your soul, your inner truth, and the complete remembrance of all your spiritual knowledge—she tells you that the sunrise every morning is your reminder to open up your gift and to radiate your light everywhere, every day, in and through all your experiences, to share it with other souls and with the earth and the universe.

Traveling within the sun ray—your special essence of light—shining and sharing your light with the world, you notice that you're now over the clearing in the forest where you began your journey of remembrance and recognition.

Floating down gently through the tops of the trees, you land softly back on the earth, knowing that the sun—the universal essence of light—is the most special and sacred place you have ever seen, the most wondrous place you have ever been, and that your soul has just taken a brief journey home to remember and renew its essence.

You embrace both the earth and the universe with open arms and an open heart, joyfully sharing the gift you have received from the sun—the gift you've given to yourself from your soul. As you share your gift of inner light, it begins to grow brighter and to radiate with its own sacred, unique light to illuminate the world.

You are a special, spiritual sun ray, and you recognize that the sacred gift you received—the treasure that you've always known is within you—is the inner light of your soul, emanating and radiating everywhere, shining brightly upon the earth, filling the world and the universe with love, peace, joy, and harmony. Let your light shine brightly.

Fantasy Friend

Remember the imaginary friend you had as a child, your special playmate who lived in a very private place inside your imagination? Even though no one else believed they were real, you knew, in a magical place in your heart and deep inside your soul, that your friend was just as real as you are.

Somehow, though, you lost touch with your special friend, but you never truly forgot them or all the good times you both shared. You think about the times they cheered you up when you felt sad and the way your friend would magically appear out of nowhere when you most needed them, or if you just wanted someone to talk to or play with.

Now, as an adult, you think about them once in a while and wonder from time to time what happened to your fantasy friend who was very real to you. Did they disappear into nothingness when you left them behind to grow up in what the adults around you said was the real world? Or did your friend grow up too, in their own special world, in the magical world that you created for them and for you?

You decide to look inside your mind to see if they're still there and, if they are, to see what happened to them. You think that maybe, if you close your eyes and allow an image of your fantasy friend to form, you could be with them again, that they can somehow be real again.

Somewhere inside yourself, you begin to think and hope—and maybe even to believe again—that your imaginary friend might have been more than a fantasy friend, that they are a special being who has the ability to magically reappear in your life, just the way they did when you were younger.

Still believing in that magical world you enjoyed and explored as a child, you know that it's always been a special part of you, and now you can remember it clearly and go there again, inside the wonderful world of your imagination where every thought and feeling and experience is real.

Remembering the way to get there, you journey joyfully into that part of yourself that you never really forgot and never truly left behind.

Calling to them with hopeful anticipation, you see your fantasy friend waiting for you, waiting ever so patiently for your return, waiting to embrace you again and share with you their companionship and love. Even though you're an adult now, they have many special things to offer and share with you.

Maybe you'll discover that they're all grown up now, too and that they've never left you, even though you may not have been aware of them for many years. Or maybe you'll find that they're just the way they were when you let your awareness of them go and that they still have the magical ability to bring the childlike wonder and joy back into your life.

As you reunite with them and renew your bond of friendship and love, they offer you a gift, a special treasure that your soul has desired for a long time.

Editor's Note

For ease of reading, the plural "they" has been used when referring to a singular person so that the words "him" or "her" and "he" or "she" do not interfere with the flow of the meditation.

Earth Energy

It's a beautiful, sunny day, and you're outside running in a wide-open, grassy expanse of earth, totally enjoying your physical exercise and the harmony you feel with your body. The blueness of the sky and the greenness of the grass surround you and envelop you.

It's just you and the sky and the earth. You feel a wonderful sense of total freedom all around you as you experience complete harmony with the sky and the air, and with the earth and the grass. Everything around you and within you is vibrantly alive, pulsing with life, and you feel more energized than you've ever felt before.

You're very aware of the rhythm of your pace, your breathing and heartbeat, and how your pace matches the energies within you and the vibrations of everything around you. You feel the energies of the earth vibrating in rhythm with your pace, in rhythm with the energies inside your physical body.

You're completely focused on and tuned into this special feeling of being at one with yourself and, at the same time, being at one with nature and in harmony with the earth.

You've been running for several miles, experiencing the joy of your freedom and movement, and your energy and the exhilaration of your physical exercise, but now you begin to slow down. Tapering off to a walk and then stopping to rest, you lie in the soft green grass, feeling your heart beat and being aware of your breathing.

Looking at the bright blueness of the cloudless sky, smelling the fresh scent of the green grass, and breathing in the pure, clean air, you again sense the harmonies all around you and within you. You sense that your inner energy is very similar to the energy within the earth.

A gentle breeze is blowing, refreshing you. You become even more aware of how the vibrations of everything around you match your own inner vibrations, and this realization inspires within you a deeper feeling of harmony and oneness with nature, a feeling of being truly connected with the earth.

You feel a strong sense of energy and vitality coming up from the earth, almost like a heartbeat. At first you think that it's your heart beating from the long run, but soon you realize it's more than that. You're feeling the energy of the earth beneath you. The earth feels as if it's alive. It has a heartbeat and breath, just like you.

Tuning in even more to the vibrant energies of the earth, you begin to recognize that the earth is a living, breathing being. Feeling the earth breathe in rhythm with your breathing and sensing its essence—its heartbeat—pulsing from within, in harmony with your heartbeat, you feel completely connected to the energy of the earth.

Feeling grounded and centered within yourself, you simultaneously sense and feel the life-force and energy of the earth beneath you— breathing, vibrant, and very much alive, just like you.

Breathe, and be at one with the earth.

Transforming Tree

You're outside enjoying an incredibly beautiful spring morning, feeling the gentle warmth of the sun on your skin and face. Breathing in the pure, clean freshness of the air, you smell the wonderful scents of the earth renewing itself in the newly-growing flowers.

You notice the greenness of the grass, bushes, and trees, and how the earth is waking up all around you, creating sparkling colors and beauty and splendor everywhere you look. You're totally enjoying the feeling of being alive on such a wonderfully beautiful, radiant day.

Everything is vibrant and new and bursting with life. It's an extraordinary day, filled with joy and sunshine and gentle warmth. Looking around you and taking it all in, you feel so very happy to be part of this glorious day, to see and experience the beauty everywhere you look.

You feel completely at one with nature, with the world around you, and you sense the world within you waking up.

The bushes and trees are covered with buds and blossoms moving in the gentle breeze; they're beginning to grow their leaves, renewing themselves from deep within.

You notice the interplay and dance of sunlight on and in and through the new greenness of the trees and bushes and flowers, how the light gently touches and caresses each bud, each blossom, each new leaf, welcoming it forth.

You see an especially beautiful tree surrounded by an aura of sunlight with blossoms that are just beginning to open up. You feel an affinity with this tree, and you're magically drawn to it. Putting your arms around the trunk, you hug it tenderly, thankful that this tree exists and that it shares its reawakening and renewal with you.

As you hug the tree, you feel your inner essence, your spirituality reawakening into the vibrant, radiant light and joy of life—beginning to blossom and grow—renewing your aliveness from deep within and opening up your soul to new levels of awareness.

You feel a special kinship and communion with the tree as it transforms itself and shares with you its essence of life from within. You know that as you share your blossoming awareness—your spiritual essence, your renewal of life and energy with the tree—you share with all of life.

But it's more than that. Just as you gave the tree a gift of love in the form of a hug, the tree has given you a special gift—a reminder of your own spiritual reawakening, your transformation and growth, your inner essence opening up and springing forth, blossoming and growing, renewing itself in your life.

Running Through the Rain

Watching the gentle rainfall through a window on a warm summer day, you remember when you were a child and you ran through the rain, catching the raindrops on your tongue and tasting their delicious wetness. You remember twirling around in circles and laughing with pure joy as the raindrops fell all around you, kissing your face and skin.

You remember standing in the mud with your bare feet, squishing the warm, gooey mud through them, and feeling the softness of the earth ooze between your toes. You remember splashing exuberantly in the puddles on the grass with total abandon to see how high the splashes would go. You remember what the rain sounded like as it touched the leaves in the trees, splattering and singing a special song to you. You remember what the sky and the clouds looked like, what the earth smelled like, and what the wind and rain felt like on your body.

Deciding to experience all of that again, you take off your shoes, fling open the door, and run outside to embrace and experience and enjoy the rain in the magical way you did when you were a child.

Running joyfully through the rain, totally experiencing and enjoying your freedom and energy, you feel the wind in your hair and the gentle touch of the breeze on your body. Turning your face up to the sky, you feel the soft kiss of the rain on your face. You feel as if you're a child again, carefree and completely happy.

Rainbow Reflections

Looking up at the sky, you notice the most beautiful rainbow you've ever seen. It's magical and mystical, with a special aura all around it, and you begin to get a sense of the vibrant energies flowing through the rainbow. Shimmering in the light reflected from the sun, it radiates and sends sparkles of light everywhere.

Standing on the ground, you somehow feel the rainbow shimmering inside you as you gaze up at it. The sparkles of light seem to invite you within the rainbow, to draw you up into and inside the rainbow.

Knowing how special and magical you really are, you know you can fly up into and through this very magical, mystical rainbow in the sky.

With one small jump, you enter into the rainbow, experiencing the awe and wonder and joy of it with every part of your being. You feel the energies of the colors vibrating all around you and through you.

Completely opening up and involving all your physical and spiritual senses in exploring and experiencing the rainbow, you know and feel the mystical magic of it with every part of your awareness. A magical, wonderful, joyful feeling enters within your body, your heart, your mind, and your soul.

Rising through each vibration of energy and color in the rainbow, you find, to your delight, that there are magical gifts and treasures, and wonderful images and feelings inside each color, just waiting for you to see them and accept them.

Taking your time, you thoroughly explore every vibration and color and open all the many special gifts and treasures you discover, as you also experience the wonderfully clear images and the joyful, vibrant feelings that the colors bring forth inside you.

Breathing in the entire essence of the rainbow within every part of you—totally immersing yourself within all the vibrations of energies and lights and colors and sounds of it—seeing, touching, tasting, smelling, and hearing the harmony and joy of it, and experiencing the radiant energies of the many soft and subtle hues and vibrations of the colors, you become the shimmering, sparkling, vibrant rainbow.

Your physical and spiritual essence, your body, mind, heart, and soul, is within every part of the rainbow, your feelings blending and blurring together, vibrating joyfully in a kaleidoscope of beautifully majestic, ethereal colors and images and feelings, radiating and emanating sparkles of light everywhere.

You feel the vibrations of the rainbow sparkling and shimmering and emanating from within your body—from within the center of your being, the very core of your soul, and radiating outward from yourself.

You're a rainbow of colors, vibrating in a magical flow and radiance of energy, expanding both inward and outward.

Rising through the mist above the rainbow into the white light of the universe, you feel the white light vibrating in harmony with your soul, in tune with your spiritual essence. You feel a love and peace and joy that is completely in harmony with your energies, and you know, with every part of your being, that you're really a rainbow.

Guardian Angel

A radiant being appears before you in a glowing ball of light that sparkles and shimmers with the ethereal essence of the universe. Stepping out of the light, you immediately recognize this beautiful being as the guardian angel who has always been with you in every moment of your life.

She* reaches forward to touch you, to embrace and hold you lovingly. As you move toward her and feel her tender touch, you are deeply moved by a very joyful and magnificent emotion that words can't describe. You feel the love and joy that emanates from her and surrounds you completely, filling you with a warmth that soothes your soul and calms your mind.

Closing your eyes, you see and remember the many times and ways, and magical moments, that your guardian angel has appeared to you and been with you, and all the ways she has helped, guided, and protected you. Very often she has spoken to you in your thoughts and created beautiful images as she danced through your dreams in sparkles and shimmers of light.

Reflecting back on the many times she has appeared in your life, you see that she has taken on many forms, some seen and some unseen. At times, she may have appeared as a person who offered you a word of kindness or encouragement. At other times you may have seen her as a beautiful flower that caught your attention and brought you enjoyment.

You may have sensed her presence in a beautiful rainbow that inspired a sense of awe and wonder and joy inside you. You may have felt her presence as a gentle whisper of the wind blowing softly on your face, or as a wonderful feeling of warmth and love, or as a gentle wave

---

* Angels can also be male or androgynous, or an ethereal essence. For purposes of clarity in this meditation, your guardian angel has been referred to as female.

of energy vibrating around you, or as a protective force that kept you safe from impending harm or danger.

You may have physically felt a soft kiss on your cheek, or a gentle brush on your shoulder, or a touch of healing to ease an ache or a pain. You may have heard her voice when she softly spoke to you, calling your name when no one was there, or you may have heard music— sounds of your soul played by her.

She may have been in the light of a person's eyes when they smiled at you, or in a sparkle of light just beyond the periphery of your vision, or in a star that twinkled at you from the universe.

See the times that she has appeared in your thoughts and dreams. See her in your intuition and insight when perhaps she offered an idea or an answer to a question, or helped you to find a solution to a problem, or gave you direction and guidance when you were troubled, or helped you find your way when you were lost.

Remember the times, inside your feelings and emotions, when she soothed you when you were sad, or cheered you up with a thought or a feeling of love that seemed to come from out of nowhere. Remember when she brought you feelings of peace and harmony when you most needed them and when she shared very special moments of joy with you.

Think about the many times that she has played inside your imagination, drifting magically through your daydreams and floating in your reveries, offering you lightheartedness, happiness, and pleasure. Remember the times she has given you very special gifts that were either tangible or intangible—ones that may have been of a physical or a spiritual nature.

Renew your deep and abiding relationship with her, knowing that your guardian angel has always been there for you and that she will always be in your life, in both the magical and the mundane moments.

Multidimensional Meadow

It's a pleasantly warm, sunny day with a gentle breeze, and you're in a field of beautiful, colorful flowers growing wild and free in an open, expansive meadow. Slowly walking among the flowers, you admire and appreciate their beauty.

Gently touching and caressing them, you sense how special and magical they are. Breathing in their pleasing fragrance as they share their inner essence with you, you know they're vibrantly alive, flowing with the natural energy and harmony of life.

After a while, you stop walking and sit in this beautiful field of flowers. You feel completely at one with and in tune with nature all around you, and you sense your awareness—your inner essence—opening up inside you in a magical, mystical way.

Sitting amidst the flowers, admiring and appreciating their gentle beauty and quiet serenity, and the vibrations of peace and harmony they offer and share with you, you hear a soft whisper in your mind and you realize that it is also in the air and all around you.

Listening, you pinpoint the source of sound, and you realize that it is coming from a flower, that the flower is talking to you, and that all the flowers are talking to one another, communicating in their special way.

At first this seems surprising, then it begins to feel perfectly natural to you. You realize that you're in a magical meadow where you can somehow hear and communicate with the world of nature, where you can talk to plants and flowers, and understand their language.

You remember that, as a child, you would often talk to the flowers and listen to them as they spoke to you.

Looking at the flower that spoke to you, you see a little ray of light emanating and radiating and sparkling from the center of it. At first you think it's a reflection of sunlight glistening from a small drop of nectar.

Looking more closely at the flower, you see what appears to be a tiny insect, then you recognize that it looks more like a fairy, reminiscent of pictures you've seen in books.

You smile to yourself, then laugh, clapping your hands with joy. The fairies you used to believe in when you were a child are *real*. You remember how you used to talk with the grass and the trees, and the flowers and the plants—how you used to play with the fairies who were your friends, how you used to dance and sing and laugh with them.

As you grew up, you placed this wonder-filled time in your memory as a magical game of make-believe, but deep inside you knew that it was more than pretend, much more than fantasy. You knew that the earth and all of nature was alive, growing and giving life, and you kept this memory in a special place inside your mind.

It has lain dormant within you, occasionally partially reawakening and gently tugging at your awareness when you admire and enjoy a flower, or when you see a beautiful, flowering bush, or when you notice how it just feels good and makes you happy to be in nature.

Or perhaps you grow a garden in your yard or in planters on your patio to remind you of the magical world of flowers and fairies you experienced as a child and can know again now—a magical world that is vibrantly alive, waiting only for you to fully remember and recognize it.

In this multidimensional meadow in your mind, you can remember and reexperience the realm of nature spirits and flower fairies who are the caregivers of the plant kingdom on earth. And in your physical world, the next time you see a flower, you can again experience and attune yourself to the magical world of nature.

Allow this meditation to first be a special, magical place in your mind—a wonderful memory reopening—and then allow it to grow into a natural state of mind. This multidimensional meadow exists in both worlds: the world within you of your spiritual, subconscious knowing and the world around you of your physical, conscious awareness.

Perhaps you'd like to plant a few flowers, to tenderly nurture them with love and care and attention the way you did when you were a child, to be in harmony and cooperation with the earth, and to remember how interconnected you are with the world of nature.

Talk to the flowers and smile at them; tune into their vibrations and listen to what the flower fairies have to say to you.

Walking Through the Woods

Imagine a very pleasant, warm summer day. You decide to go for a walk through the woods to renew your relationship with nature and to reconnect with the earth—to appreciate its beauty and to experience the joy and harmony of the earth with the universe. Deep inside yourself, you know that you're part of that special connection and you'd like to feel that again.

The day is filled with the quiet sounds of nature; you feel and hear the gentle breeze as it touches you and moves softly through the leaves of the trees in the forest just ahead of you. Walking toward the trees, you feel the warmth of the sun and begin to reexperience the sense of aliveness and vibrancy that being in nature brings you.

Breathing in deeply, you feel the pure, clean air circulate through your lungs, revitalizing and rejuvenating every part of your mind and your body. As this energy flows through your body, you feel lighter and happier. As it flows through your mind, all your cares and worries slip away as you enjoy this beautiful day, this wonderful walk through nature.

Entering the forest, you notice how the sunshine sparkles through the tops of the trees, creating shafts and streams of light from the sky to the earth, and you see how the breeze interacts with the leaves and plays with patterns on the forest floor. You notice how intricate the patterns are, and how they're constantly moving and changing.

Walking through the open, airy forest, you notice how quiet it is inside the forest and how peaceful it is. You begin to enter a meditative frame of mind, a special, serene place within yourself where you feel completely comfortable and natural.

You see a tall, majestic tree in the center of a clearing up ahead. The sunlight sparkles and shimmers all around the tree as it beckons you forth, inviting you in and welcoming you as if you are an old and dear friend. You know that you've been here before—in your thoughts and in your dreams.

Feeling perfectly at home and in tune with yourself, you walk slowly, thoughtfully, into the clearing. Sitting quietly on the soft ground next to the tree, enjoying the feeling of peace and harmony within you and all around you, you begin to remember.

The gentle breeze creates a light, musical sound that vibrates in harmony within your mind as the wind blows softly through the leaves of the tree. Leaning up against the tree, you close your eyes, listening to your thoughts and watching their images move in your mind.

The leaves whisper in the wind and through your mind, sharing the secrets of nature and the knowledge of the universe. Somehow you know that you can communicate with the tree, and you listen as it tells you about its connection with the earth and the universe, about how its roots are connected to the earth as its branches reach toward the sky, toward the universe.

The tree speaks to you of the harmony that is within nature, the harmony that the earth and the universe share, the harmony that you share between your physical self and your spiritual self. It tells you that the universe is within you and that you are the universe, expressing your spiritual nature—your true self—in earthly form.

As you listen and remember, you begin to reunite with yourself, joining your physical awareness with your spiritual essence, feeling all the joy and harmony that this brings within you.

After a while, you open your eyes. Looking up at the sky, you see a few puffy white clouds floating by, and you notice how blue and expansive the sky is. It seems to go on forever, beyond the horizon into the universe and even farther than that into infinity.

The sky has an ethereal quality—a magical, mystical essence that you know within your mind, yet can't describe with words—a majesty that you've known before but haven't experienced for a while.

Breathing in deeply, you absorb the depth of the blueness within yourself; the color fills you with a wonderful feeling of peace and awareness, with a deep inner sense of remembrance and knowing.

Standing up, you feel as if you could reach up through the sky and touch the universe. Stretching your arms upward in an open embrace toward the sky, you feel a magical surge of energy and power inside you, knowing that you're part of the earth and the universe.

You remember and become fully aware of how awesome the world really is, and you rediscover how awesome you really are; you fully sense your true spiritual nature, and the knowledge and power of the universe opening up within you.

You decide to continue walking, to explore everything you see, and to experience and understand both the world within you and the world around you. Your pace is in rhythm with your mind's awareness that has opened up completely.

Reaching the edge of the forest, you turn and look back, knowing that you've just taken a wonderful walk through the woods. You've remembered the truth of your spiritual nature and reunited with yourself as the tree shared its true nature and its treasures of knowledge with you. You've reconnected with the earth and reexperienced the joy and harmony of the earth with the universe—the harmony of your physical self with your spiritual self.

As you continue forward in your life, you carry with you the special knowledge that you're truly a spiritual being and that you are connected in a very special way with both the earth and the universe.

Treasures of the Tree

Deep within a secluded glen, you happen upon an old gnome guarding a mysterious and majestic tree. You sense that this tree is very special; it feels familiar to you, as if you've somehow touched this tree before, or perhaps this tree has joined its soul with yours at some time in the past. The gnome comes forward to greet you, telling you that he has been caring for this tree while it awaited your return.

Somewhere in your soul's knowing, a memory begins to stir and you remember the bond and connection you've formed with this tree in long-ago ages past, and most recently in this lifetime in your childhood friendship with all of the nature spirits and flower fairies, and especially with this tree who offered you comfort and clarity—this tree who was your companion and confidant—the one you whispered all your secrets to and showed all the dreams and hopes in your heart.

You've returned now to your special friend—to this tree—and you once again sit beneath it and lean back against it, sharing what is inside your soul and listening to all that the tree has to share with you.

AUTHOR'S NOTE

Perhaps you have a special tree, just as this tree is my special, treasured tree. It is a real tree in a real place, and I visit it often, renewing my bond with it and the special connection that my soul shares with this tree.

If you don't have a special tree somewhere in your soul's memory or someplace in your childhood, you can find your treasured tree—the one your soul resonates with. It is waiting for you, calling to you and beckoning you, wanting to find you just as much as you want to find your tree and to connect your spirits together.

You will locate your tree in a sacred site of energy and nature that is a special place for you. Perhaps it is in the woods close to your home, or in a forest preserve, or in your yard, or perhaps it exists in your mind or in your memory.

Go there and choose your tree carefully by touching and feeling and sensing the energy and essence of individual trees. You will begin to notice the difference between them. Trees are just as much alive as you are. They have a soul and life-force all their own, just like you and me. Each tree has its own unique personality and vibration.

When you've found a tree that you resonate with—one that is in harmony with your soul—sit beneath it, leaning up against it. Be in a gentle, quiet frame of mind; open up your heart and meditate. Join your heart with its essence, intertwine your soul with its spirit—and listen with your mind. The tree will whisper to you in your heart and mind—through your thoughts and feelings—and you can communicate with your special tree in the same manner.

When you've finished meditating, thank your tree for sharing its wisdom and knowledge and the secrets of nature with you, and for listening to you and innately knowing what is inside you. Be aware of the gifts and treasures that your tree has given you, just as you've given to your tree. Hug your tree with love. You will feel the love from the tree that emanates back to you.

You've formed and forged a bond with this special tree, intertwining your souls. As you begin to walk away, you turn to look at your tree— your special friend now—and you know that you can come to your tree, both physically and in your mind, at any time to meditate, to refresh and replenish your spirit, and to achieve clarity and inner knowing.

As you look at your tree, you notice that a nature spirit—perhaps a gnome or a deva or an angel—is standing beside your tree and will care for it until you return. You also know that this nature spirit is the essence of your tree—its life-source and soul.

Journey Into Yourself

Feel yourself beginning to drift pleasantly and easily. You are about to enter a magical realm of your mind's memories. You experience a feeling of letting go, of beginning to drift through the passage of time, of becoming more in perfect harmony with yourself. You feel in tune with yourself, with every part of you.

As you drift gently and easily back through time, remember a pleasant, happy, carefree time when you were a child. Just allow a memory to surface. As you recall a pleasant, happy memory, you automatically smile, and you feel the joy within yourself.

As a child, you had many happy and pleasant dreams and experiences. Perhaps in one of your dreams or experiences, you were walking barefoot in the sand along the shore by the water's edge. Remember what that feels like. Feel the warm sun shining on your skin and a gentle, cool breeze that balances the warmth of the sun. Remember the scent of the water and the spray from the waves that softly touched you. Perhaps there is a beautiful lighthouse in the distance.

Listen to the sound of seagulls. Looking up at the sky, you see them flying and floating gracefully through the air. It seems to you that they are laughing. They are happy to be by the water and are expressing their joy. As this dream or experience continues to flow, you continue to go softly into the magical land of gentle dreams, to that carefree, innocent, joyous part of you—the part of you that is very special and sacred—to the magical essence of your inner child.

Connect now with your inner child, with that joyful, wonderful, innocent part of you. You may wish to communicate with your inner child or to embrace your inner child with love, experiencing the joy of remembering who you were and experiencing the incredible healing power of love that your inner child has within—the healing love that your inner child wishes to share with you. Take some time now to just be with your inner child, to talk with him or her, or to commune silently as you reconnect with this very special part of you.

Your inner child has a gift to give you. Perhaps it is something intangible—a word, a phrase, a memory, or maybe it is a symbolic object that means something very special to you.

As you accept the gift that is lovingly given to you, you bring it close to your breast, to your heart, so that you may keep it always in a special place of love within you. If it is a gift that your inner child would like for you to share, acknowledge it with love and tell your inner child that you will be most happy to share it.

Now it is time for you to leave, to continue following the dream. There is another dream within the dream—the dream of your eternal self. As your dream progresses, you bid your inner child good-bye, promising you will return.

Continuing to walk along the water's edge, listening to the waves as they gently touch the shore, you become aware that in the innocence of a child there is the eternal wisdom and strength of the universe.

The dream beckons you to a river—the river of life—through the realms of many, many yesterdays, through the waters of the timeless essence of life itself. You enter the water, knowing that you're perfectly safe, and begin to float upon and to move through the waters of life, going easily into and with the flow, to the source of life, to the source of your soul.

As you travel gently, easily, to the source, to the wellspring of life eternal, you notice many magical and wonderful things along the way. But knowing that you are on a specific journey at this moment, you stay with the flow. You realize that you can return to explore and experience anything you see at another time, whenever you wish.

Continuing to flow gently and easily, you arrive at the source. Breathe the air and notice what it smells like. Feel the breeze and listen to any quiet and gentle sounds that you may hear.

With the feelings of wonderment and joy that you are experiencing here, you also notice an exhilaration—a feeling of strength and wisdom. You know, somehow, that this is the dwelling place of your higher self, the very highest aspect of your being. You know that you are visiting the home of your soul and that this is where your higher self resides— the sage, the counselor, the friend who watches over you and helps you, guides you, and protects you—your most special and wonderful friend.

Your higher self has been waiting for you and now appears and comes forward to greet you and to embrace you lovingly. You feel an incredible joy and love that words cannot truly describe.

You know that you've traveled through all of eternity with him or her. Your higher self has many things to say to you and to share with you. Reunite with the most spiritual and knowledgeable part of yourself. Take all the time you need to both commune and communicate with the eternal essence of yourself.

Your higher self also has a special gift to give you. As you accept this gift in gratitude and reverence, you know and completely understand the meaning and purpose of this priceless gift. You hold it close to your heart, knowing that it is a profound treasure.

You thank your higher self and give him or her a gift in return. Your higher self smiles and accepts your gift with love, knowing that it is given from your soul; it is a gift that when shared with your higher self is also a gift that you give to yourself. Perhaps it is a promise; perhaps it is a sacred memento of a special time that you remember.

As you turn to leave, to continue your journey through this dream within a dream, you know that this dream is very real and is a magical, mystical part of your life. You leave with an understanding that you can return here at any time you wish, now that you remember the way here.

The dream begins to flow into the river of life with its many streams and its eternal waters. As you begin to awaken from this dream, you see yourself again walking along the water's edge.

As this dream begins to flow into another dream, the recognition of yet another dream within a dream appears to you, and you know that this is the dream of life, for life is really just a dream that flows eternally. You're aware that it's sometimes difficult to realize just where and when one dream ends and another begins.

You realize that your present life seems like another dream that flows endlessly from its source, and that what you perceive to be reality blends into the dream as your dreams create your reality that you call life. You begin to wonder whether you're dreaming your current life.

This thought is intriguing, but for now, it's time to return to the dream that you call your life. As you follow one of the streams within the river of life, it returns you to where you began this most special journey into yourself.

As you let the dreamer within you awaken, you reflect on everything you've experienced, bringing with you all the special gifts that your inner child and your higher self have given you.

Travels of Time

You find yourself walking with a spiritual guide or a master in a universal dimension. As you talk and walk, you begin to recognize this being as a very special friend—a soul companion (or perhaps he or she is your higher self or the essence of your soul)—that you've traveled with many times before, seeking and sharing knowledge. As you open the vibrations of your soul, you remember.

In this special self-guided meditation, draw an image and a feeling of walking with a very knowledgeable master, one who you begin to realize and recognize is an old friend. You become aware that the two of you are equals, and you can both share your knowledge with one another. Travel with this person to find your truth.

Feast of the Seven Senses

The invitation that arrived in the mail this morning simply and mysteriously read, "You're invited to share a magical meal of knowledge with some very special guests. Come as you are to the center of the forest. There you will see a clearing and a magnificent feast set before you."

Naturally curious and wondering what this is all about, thinking that it's probably a practical joke or a prank from a friend or co-worker, you decide to show up at this picnic, or whatever it is, but you haven't got a clue as to where to find this place. A voice from out of nowhere, seemingly from the thin air, whispers to you, "To find this magical place, follow where your mind leads you."

You feel yourself being drawn to a scene where you will experience this "magical" meal of knowledge—a feast of your senses, a feast of your soul.

Imagine a forest scene or some type of natural setting where your senses can show you what they're saying, where you can see what they want to share with you, and where you can hear what they've been whispering to you in all your thoughts, dreams, feelings, insights, intuitions, memories, and imagination. Hear and listen to them as they speak, as they tell you how they can express themselves fully and freely.

As you open up your physical, psychic (mental), and spiritual senses—enhancing them and blending them together—each sense speaks of its special qualities, of the limits it experiences as a single sense and the unlimited possibilities and powers it possesses when combined with all your other senses.

Review each sense, seeing its special qualities but limited abilities when used separately. Allow each sense to tell you what is possible and what it can achieve when it combines with each of your other senses to use their properties together, sharing with one another.

Looking around the forest scene at the feast that is set before you, your eyes begin to speak. See what they have to say and to show you. See what they want to share with you. See what they have to give you and offer to you.

Listening to the sounds around you, to the wind as it whispers through the woods, your ears begin to speak. Hear what they have to say and to show you. Hear your inner voice. Hear what your sense of listening wants to share with you.

Touching the food and picking it up with your fingers, your feelings begin to speak of textures and vibrations of both seen and unseen energies, of your experiences and emotions, reminding you that food is knowledge—a feast of the gods. As you look at the huge array of knowledge that is set before you on this table, you see that it is a smorgasbord for your soul to choose from. You may partake of whatever wisdom you desire and need at this particular time in your life.

Putting the food in your mouth and savoring its texture, its deliciousness and succulent juiciness, your taste buds tell you about the many flavors in your life, the variety and quality of all the events that happen to you, and the emotions you feel as you both sense them within and experience them in your life. Taste all your feelings, emotions, and experiences with every part of your soul.

Smelling the wonderful aroma of the food and breathing in the pure, clean air around you, your sense of smell tells you of your unique ability to sense and sniff out vibrations in the air around you, to sense and know of experiences and changes before they occur, and to be aware of and know their full range as they are happening.

Your sense of smell asks you to breathe in the full essence and aroma of life, of all your everyday experiences and activities, to know how special and magical they truly are and to become aware of all the miracles you've created and can create now, simply by using your senses together.

Each sense expresses its sadness at its separateness and voices its desire to join together with all its interrelated senses, to share its unique abilities and thus enhance and add to the depth, scope, and full range of each and all your senses, thereby increasing and expanding the depth and scope of all your experiences.

All your senses—and your inner knowing—tell you how, as a child, you did this naturally and automatically, but somehow you outgrew this ability or left it behind to lie dormant and unused; you realize you've remained unaware of this ability you've always had within you, until now.

Your senses tell you of how you filtered this awareness and put it outside of yourself as you grew up and began to explore the outside world. They remind you of all the magic you used to know, and can know again, if you'll open up all your senses and use them together, if you'll allow yourself to open up all your inner knowings and to reclaim all the wisdom you have within yourself.

You decide to open up, explore, and experience the full range of all your senses, using them together in a physical, psychic, and spiritual way.

Your senses speak to you again. This time your sixth (psychic) and seventh (spiritual) senses chime in to have their say—sharing the special knowledge that is already inside you, showing you everything that is possible, everything that is within your reach to remember, to know and achieve, when you open up all your seven senses and use them in harmony.

Secluded Serenity

Create an image of a peaceful, calm pool of water in a secluded cove. Perhaps there's a small waterfall and you can listen to the soft sound. See the lush greens and flowering bushes that surround you and are comforting.

See the trees. Perhaps there's a gentle swaying palm tree or a weeping willow tree that moves gracefully in the gentle breeze as its branches touch the water.

This is a perfectly peaceful place in nature, a quiet, soothing, relaxing, safe place where you can be alone—a sanctuary all your own.

It's beautiful and untouched; no one has ever been here before. You're the first and only person to have set foot here. It's a sacred space that you can experience and enjoy.

It's a special place where you can rejuvenate your body, a serene place where you can refresh your mind and replenish the spiritual energies of your soul.

There's a magical essence in this place of secluded serenity, a mystical feel and sense to this beautiful place in nature. It has an aura about it, an ambiance and charm that you resonate perfectly to with every part of you.

Feel the tranquillity of this secluded place in nature nurture your mind and body, and nourish your soul.

Take a deep breath and relax completely. Just be. Let your mind be still, free from all the cares and worries of the outside world.

This is your special, private place—your place of secluded serenity—a paradise that you share with the natural wonders and beauties of the earth.

Tapestry of Truth

You receive a special-delivery gift in the mail. The package is large and soft, wrapped in white paper, and tied with coarse threads of twine. You have no idea who sent it to you, and you open it eagerly, wondering what it is.

Inside is a beautiful tapestry with many colorful images woven in and through the design. The pattern is intricate and detailed; the images are very descriptive. Looking at it more closely, you realize that you're looking at a tapestry of time showing scenes that are vaguely familiar, and then you begin to recognize the pattern and the images.

The tapestry reveals the pictures in your mind—the images of your thoughts, feelings, experiences, and dreams. It is a tapestry of truth, all about your life, the threads magically interwoven with the images of your life, merging the physical and spiritual worlds. One of the many things it shows you is your search for knowledge and your quest for truth.

You hang the tapestry in a special place in your home and study the images. The tapestry is timeless, showing scenes from the past, present, and future, bringing them together and blending them into the ever-present moment of here and now.

Sometimes the images are still, at other times they move. Every time you look at the tapestry, you see something new and different. It's fascinating to watch. Events seem to be happening and changing all the time, pictures appearing and disappearing, yet the design and pattern always remain interrelated and connected.

Sometimes the images blur together, as if they're occurring simultaneously. Sometimes they appear as silhouettes, echoing one another. And at other times, they run side by side, paralleling and mirroring each other. Sometimes the parallels merge, sometimes they go entirely different ways.

At times, the picture draws you within, and you're inside the images and experiencing the scenes that the tapestry depicts. These events are the threads of your life, showing you the patterns and places inside your soul, intricately interwoven and filled with wonder.

As you go inside the images of this magical, mystical tapestry, you fully understand each and every experience, and each and every thought and feeling that is woven into and through the fabric of your life.

Alternate Avenues

Have you ever wondered where your choices, thoughts, and feelings go when you don't actively pursue them and make them real in the physical, three-dimensional world? They don't cease to exist; you create them somewhere else and experience them in another realm of reality beyond your conscious mind. This meditation shows you how to reach into those realms of reality to explore and see for yourself all the many facets and expressions of your choices, thoughts, and feelings.

You're standing at a crossroads that leads four ways. It seems to be a crossroads of choices, and farther up ahead, in the distance, you see even more crossroads. Looking near-sightedly, right in front of you, you wonder what will happen on each road should you decide to travel in that direction. There are no signposts, and you don't have a road map.

At the moment, you haven't got a clue which way to go or how to proceed. All you have is a choice that you must make, and you know that each road will take you in a vastly different direction into your experience, and that up ahead are many twists and turns.

You wish you could somehow travel all the roads simultaneously to see where they will lead, where your choice will take you, and what experiences you'll have on each particular road, but you know that you can commit to only one road. Then you remember the magic of your mind, and you know that you can travel each alternate avenue to see and know and experience what will happen if you follow that path.

Suddenly you laugh to yourself, knowing that whatever choice you make and whatever road you decide to travel is always the right choice, the right path. You also know that your choice isn't limited to one road, that your choice can travel each road simultaneously, yet a bit differently, arriving at its individual outcome, and that you can be aware of each experience on every road simply by focusing your attention there. You realize that you could go a little out of your mind with this and end up here, there, and everywhere, maybe at the same time and even in the same place, but in a different vibration of energy.

To be in what everyone says is the "real world," you can make only one choice and travel one road at a time. You know this isn't true—that this is merely how people keep structure in their lives by isolating each experience into a separate event—though for the moment you'll buy into that linear and limiting belief.

But it feels so stifling that you immediately change your mind because you want to explore your choices completely; you want to be adventuresome and know the full range of your experiences and gather all the information you can discover about the choice you're going to make, or a choice you've already made.

You decide to travel each road to see where your choice will lead you once you take action and commit to it in your physical reality. Joyfully, you step bravely onto the path before you, traveling in many directions simultaneously and exploring the myriad manifestations of your choice.

After seeing how your choice expresses itself in various forms and vibrations of your experiences, and the events you've caused to occur and set into motion, you center yourself into the here and now to review the experiences you've encountered and to contemplate the knowledge, awareness, and insights you've received.

This gives you a road map of many directions and provides you with a wonderful, innate sense of knowing; it enables you to choose wisely, knowing that all you have to do is change your focus of awareness and attention—your perception and perspectives—and your choice will show itself differently in all the avenues and various aspects of your life.

You smile to yourself, knowing that in the real world, all your choices are happening simultaneously, that you vibrate to and resonate with every experience on many levels of your awareness, and that this is how you draw changes and chances, and coincidences and synchronicity into your life—that this is the real way that all your experiences manifest and show and express themselves.

You think about how freeing and empowering this is—being aware of all your experiences in every dimension and vibration of your reality, and how they're all intricately connected and intertwined with your present, with the here and now. You're just simply aware of them now, where they previously escaped your attention before.

You feel exhilarated and happy, knowing that you can see through the illusions of your physical reality—of the three-dimensional world—into your true reality. You know that your thoughts don't ever disappear or go into nothingness; they reappear in another vibration and frequency of energy, and in a different expression—perhaps even in another dimension or a parallel place—and that all you need to do is to tune into them to be aware of them.

Sometimes in the past, when you bought into limited, linear beliefs, you couldn't see and know all the many pieces and parts of your experiences with your physical awareness, yet the essence of them was always with you, kept within your inner knowing by your spiritual self.

Deep inside you, you also know that all your choices—every decision you've made throughout your entire lifetime and your soul's entire existence—always exists, traveling its own road and having its own experiences, reappearing in your life in another form, another expression of itself, when it gathers the appropriate, interrelated energy vibrations, through your focus of awareness and attention, drawn by your current experiences and choices.

Part
Four

Mystical
Meditations

Part Four centers on the theme of reawakening to your true self and remembering your spiritual knowledge. As the mystical meditations and musings move gently through your thoughts and step softly through your soul, you'll see your mind opening up and expanding into ever-widening and broader horizons, and you'll experience your soul stretching to new heights of awareness and enlightenment.

These meditations invite you to travel further than the center of yourself and deeper within to the very core of your being, to touch and fully experience your essence, to journey above and beyond yourself into your true spiritual nature, into the multidimensionality of your soul. They hold the promise of growing your mind and your soul, if you will look into your mind to recognize the light within you and see into your soul to remember who you really are.

Moonbeam Magic

You wake up in the middle of the night, in the middle of a dream, and look out the window. It's a starry night with a luminous full moon.

Looking up at the universe, you see the aura around the moon and notice rays of light emanating and radiating from the moon and the stars, reflecting the light of the universe.

The rays of light appear to be moonbeams of magic that sparkle and shimmer with an ethereal energy essence.

You feel as if you could magically travel a moonbeam into the universe. You've been on an inner journey for a while now in your life, and you know that this is entirely possible.

You think about the path you're traveling in your mystical search for truth, your quest for knowledge.

You want to know the infinite awareness of your mind and the vastness of your spiritual knowledge, and the universe seems to be the best place to expand your self-discovery.

Stretching, you decide to travel a moonbeam into the universe, to explore the infinite reaches of your mind, and to experience and know the mysteries of the universe.

With that thought, you find yourself riding on a beam of light, going into the universe and beyond, exploring the openness of your mind and the universe.

Spiritual Storyteller

You notice a group of people gathered around someone in a park. Interested in what is going on, you join the crowd and work your way up to the front. There you see an old man who is telling stories, wonderful parables and proverbs that inspire musings and messages as they create images and draw symbols that form into moving pictures in your mind.

He's very eloquent and articulate. As his words weave around you, entering into your imagination and through your awareness, they spin into meanings that at first you may barely comprehend with your conscious mind, but somewhere inside you, you understand. You know.

Listening to his magical, mystical stories and allowing them to take you into a special world of knowing within yourself, you begin to recognize the metaphysical meanings in the words he speaks.

You listen more attentively, focusing on his words, hearing with your mind as he speaks, elucidating the knowing that is already within you, helping you to recognize and remember your own spiritual knowledge.

His words weave a tapestry of truth, magically blending the physical and the spiritual worlds, bringing them both together. You realize that you're listening to a master storyteller—a true teacher.

Inspired and intrigued by the stories he tells, you want to learn so much more. It seems that he knows everything there is to know about everything.

It appears that he is speaking directly to you now, somehow knowing what's inside your heart, what you need to hear, and the answers you want to know. At times, he becomes quiet.

While you may think it's because he's gathering his thoughts, it's because he wisely knows that silence holds your answers, and he wants you to seek within yourself for the truth.

As you listen within, you begin to hear your own inner voice in the silence that blends with his as it becomes your voice that you're listening to.

You become aware that you're hearing the stories of your own spiritual knowing, and that this spiritual storyteller is your inner storyteller, your spiritual self, at first whispering softly to you in your thoughts, feelings, and dreams, but the more you listen, the more you hear and the more you know.

Energy Essence

You feel as if you're wandering through a misty maze in search of something special. It's just a vague feeling for the moment, and you're not quite sure what you're looking for, but know you'll recognize it immediately when you find it.

It has something to do with your truth, your spiritual knowledge, and your inner essence. Perhaps you're in search of the meaning and purpose in your life, or a special knowing somewhere inside your soul. It feels as if something is missing or misplaced, yet you know you can find it; you can remember it.

You feel as if you're on a wonderful adventure that will either lead you into the path you've chosen to follow, or will show you the way to continue on the path that you already journey upon.

You begin to look inside your mind, peering into almost-forgotten dreams and misty memories, searching for an image, a clue, a doorway, or a window—a way to remember.

You begin to get clearer on what you're searching for. What you're looking for is the answer to something you've pondered and puzzled over for many years, perhaps many lifetimes.

You want to know who you really are and why you are here. You're looking for the realness in life, for the meaning and purpose, and for what you are meant to do with your life. But you know it goes much deeper than that.

You realize that you are looking for your spiritual essence, for the knowledge and truth inside you. You're looking for yourself—your soul. You quiet your conscious mind and go within the stillness of yourself, knowing that the answers you seek are there.

The image and thought sparkles into your awareness and suddenly you know. Your answer appears as if by magic, and you laugh with the pure joy and exhilaration of finding something you've always known but have temporarily forgotten. In a sacred place inside your soul, you remember who you really are and why you are here now. You remember your soul's purpose.

With this remembrance comes the complete awareness of your true spiritual nature, and you reunite with yourself, gently wrapping the essence of your soul around you. It feels as if you are being embraced with the gentleness and love of your true spiritual self, as if you are coming home. You know that you've found yourself and given yourself a very special gift.

You've found what you've been searching for—your true spiritual nature. At the same time, you remember all your spiritual knowledge.

With this awareness, you know that you can fully express the pure energy of your soul and share your spiritual knowledge in every moment, as the light of your soul shines brightly and is reflected in every emotion and experience in your life.

Web of the Worlds

Imagine that there are invisible bonds—strands of light moving in all directions—connecting you to the worlds above you, around you, and below you, and that you are standing in the center of this web of worlds.

Imagine that the web is multidimensional, gently rising above you, quietly expanding all around you, and falling softly below you. Experience yourself as being an integral part of this web. Feel your energy as it flows freely all around you, above you, and below you.

Imagine yourself exploring all the infinite reaches of this whole web. See yourself visiting and exploring higher levels of existence and awareness in the universe above you.

Notice what colors you see, if any. Notice shapes, sounds, and textures if they are there. You have great freedom of movement, so explore as freely as you would like.

Imagine yourself visiting the realm of the world below you, deep into the center of the earth, into its core, its essence, its being. Again, notice what colors you see, if any. Notice shapes, sounds, and textures if they are there. Explore and experience everything that is there.

Imagine yourself visiting the world all around you, in every direction as far as you can see, and even farther than that. Again, notice what colors you see, if any. Notice shapes, sounds, and textures if they are there. Explore and experience everything that is there.

Imagine yourself visiting any dimension of time, space, matter, and motion that you would like. See and feel and experience everything that is there, knowing that you are connected with all the places you choose to visit in this web of worlds that are joined together with the essence of you.

Setting Your Spirit Free

Walking in a magical field and listening to your thoughts, you know that your true nature is that of a free spirit, dressed in a physical body. Your soul isn't limited in any way by physical energies, and you know you can expand your awareness and transcend the limits and restrictions of physical energies.

You know that your soul vibrates to spiritual and universal energies, in tune with nature and the universe, moving in rhythm with knowledge and awareness, in harmony with light. Your soul is the universal energy of light, and you know that you can feel and experience your spirit in its pure energy form.

Listening to your thoughts, you compare your soul to a butterfly that's free, moving on wings of spiritual and universal energies. You know that you can unwrap the physical cocoon of earthly energies and break through the paper-like shell of limited consciousness to open up your awareness and set your spirit free.

A movement in a nearby bush catches your attention. You see a beautiful butterfly emerging from its golden chrysalis. Watching its birth, you realize that you're seeing something very special and magical.

The butterfly has just emerged into the light and is beginning to open its wings to fly, to explore its new life as a transformed being— as a free spirit. As the butterfly spreads its wings, they shimmer in the sunlight, and you realize that, in essence, you are very much like the butterfly.

You feel at one with it and in harmony with the world around you and within you. You begin to understand what the butterfly feels like as it frees itself and begins to fly, floating on natural currents of air, enjoying the light of the sunshine all around it, rising and soaring into the sky and through the clouds.

You feel as if you could rise and soar with the butterfly, in harmony with air and light. You feel as if you could rise and soar into the universe, transcending physical boundaries and limits, moving upward through the clouds into the light of your spiritual energies. You feel as if you could rise even higher into universal energies, where your soul is open and free in its true form.

Becoming more in tune with the energies of the butterfly—with the energies of your spiritual nature—you feel as if you are the butterfly, and you understand its natural harmony with the earth and the universe.

Simultaneously you become aware of your natural harmony with the earth and the universe; you become aware that you can transcend earthly energies and flow into universal energies of awareness and light.

You begin to feel yourself opening up and expanding through the energies of your physical reality, transforming yourself into the vibration of your spiritual self.

Blending into your spiritual awareness, you begin to feel even more open and expansive and free, much as you imagine the butterfly felt when it peered through and released itself from its transparent, paper-like cocoon.

Flowing and floating upward into higher vibrations of awareness and light, you become in tune with your spiritual energies, and you feel the essence of your soul. As you experience this, you feel yourself—your awareness—blending into the energies of the universe, in harmony with the earth.

As the butterfly continues to float and fly, you feel yourself floating even higher, emerging and expanding into knowledge and light. The butterfly is free—flying, soaring above the earth—and you feel just as free.

You're free of the clouds of physical energies; you've emerged into the energy of your soul. You feel your spirit begin to fly and soar and expand into ever-higher realms and realities of knowledge and awareness and light.

Flying and soaring upward, higher and higher, you feel the freedom of knowledge and the light of awareness. Floating on natural currents of air and energy, you feel your spirit becoming more and more free.

As you continue to rise into the true awareness of your spirit, you see sparkles of light—rays of sunshine and the radiance of stars—that illuminate the sky. They feel vibrant and peaceful and nourishing as they shower you with awareness, as they shower the earth with light.

Absorbing the light and energy, you feel very vibrant and peaceful and nourished from the universe and from within yourself, knowing that you're really a free spirit, and that you're experiencing the energies of the true nature of your soul.

You feel illuminated with the energy of the universe, with the light of sunshine and the vibrant radiance of the stars—with the energy of your inner knowing and the light of your spiritual awareness.

You continue to fly and soar upward, higher and higher, becoming more and more free—transcending the earthly pull of physical energies, expanding into ever-widening horizons of true knowledge and awareness—flying on wings of illumination and light.

Your spirit is free, flying and soaring and expanding into the universe, moving with the motion and rhythm of knowledge and awareness and light.

AUTHOR'S NOTE

While this meditation is designed to help you to really *know* and *feel* that your true nature is that of a free spirit, that you are a spiritual being, and that you are more than your physical self, it can also be used as a takeoff point for consciously experiencing astral projection—an out-of-body experience—that occurs naturally every night as you sleep.

This meditation can take you even higher than the astral realms into the etheric and divine realms of your soul, to explore the multidimensionality of your spirit.

School of Spirituality

Earth is like a school where you learn and are tested through your physical experiences, where you advance and evolve your soul. The universe is also a school where you can study spirituality, where there are light teachers who can help you learn anything you want to know.

You think about how you'd like to find out more about your true spiritual nature, about how you'd like to be able to better prepare yourself for the daily tests you take on earth.

Somewhere in your mind you've often wished that there was a school—a higher place of learning where you could take classes that would help you tremendously in your self-discovery and spiritual growth.

The School of Spirituality is a place that exists in the universe, a place where you can remember and rediscover your spiritual knowledge and find answers to all your questions.

The curriculum is varied and interesting. There are classes that can expand your awareness and inner knowing. Weekend workshops are offered in any subject you want to know more about.

You can attend special seminars to learn about the spiritual perspectives of living in a physical body. You can take an art appreciation class to see how you really create your own reality and to learn how to draw more magic into all your experiences on earth. You can meet other students and form discussion/study groups with them. The possibilities are endless.

Though this seems to be a perfect place to study and learn, to grow your soul, you feel a bit reluctant because there are a few basic required courses. Since your soul is grounded in a physical body, you have to take classes in Time and Space, Reality Awareness, and Energy and Matter to completely comprehend the concepts and to understand the relationship of these subjects on both a physical and a spiritual level, to see how they're intertwined and how the vibrations interact with and influence each other. Then you have to incorporate this knowledge into all your day-to-day activities by expressing it through your experiences.

To graduate your soul, you have to write a master's thesis on the topic of Synchronicity and the Simultaneous Realm of Here and Now. Until you've advanced yourself above and beyond the universe, which you've heard takes a few millennia, you still have to take spiritual tests in an earthly dimension.

So while it may appear that you're right back where you started (earth), you think about all you can learn at the School of Spirituality, and you do want to attend and get a higher education that will help you evolve your soul and show you how to pass your earthly and spiritual tests in a better way, with more understanding and insight.

You decide to go for it. Maybe it's really just a dream or a parallel place in your mind, and you go there every night anyway when you think you're asleep, so it would be more fun to become conscious of it.

The more you think about it, the more the idea appeals to you. You grab your journal and your super-special pencil that writes in both worlds, and you appear on campus, ready to explore this higher realm of learning and awareness, to evolve and advance your soul.

Simply create an image of a university in your mind, place yourself in the picture, follow the flow of your thoughts, and see what happens.

Metaphysical Master

In what appears to be a dream within a dream, a metaphysical master speaks your name and gives you a small yellow rosebud that is just beginning to open up.

The stem is free from thorns, and the leaves are green and healthy. Holding it gently in your hand between your thumb and forefinger, and turning the rosebud around slowly, looking at every part of it, you admire its beauty, its perfect symmetry and balance. Even though small, the rosebud is perfectly formed.

With your other hand, you touch it lovingly, caressing it, feeling its velvety softness and its silky smoothness. Raising it to your nose, you sniff its fragrant, pleasing aroma. Holding it gently, cradling the bud in the palm of your hand, you realize that this is a very special gift, and you thank him for sharing it with you.

You know that you need to care for the rosebud tenderly, to nurture it with love and to nourish it with the energies of the universe. You place it in a vase of water and put the vase in an open, sunny window.

There is a hope in your heart that the stem will root and that you'll be able to plant it, watching it grow into a beautiful rosebush and then into a garden. Knowing that this rosebud is very magical, you realize that this is possible.

The metaphysical master seems to know your thoughts. He smiles at you and asks you to meditate on the rosebud every day, watching it open up and unfold, petal by petal, as it reaches for the sun. He asks you to do the same, to open up your mind and reach for the light of knowledge.

He asks you to notice how a dewdrop gently nourishes the bud in the early morning hours, and how it gradually opens up and blooms into a very beautiful rose in the light of day and the warmth of the sun.

He asks you to do the same, to nourish your mind with the energies of the universe, and to see your inner awareness expand and grow and bloom into a beautiful garden of spiritual knowledge.

You wake up from this dream with the scent of roses around you, and perhaps you notice a few petals on your pillow.

Just a few thoughts for you to ponder: Maybe the yellow rosebud you imagined and created at the beginning of this book—when you were learning the language of your mind and starting to grow your imagination and open up your inner knowing—is the same rosebud the metaphysical master has given you in this meditation.

And maybe this meditation, or perhaps all of life, is really just a dream, and you are your own teacher; you are the metaphysical master.

Light Library

You see a spiral stairway composed of rays of light shimmering into the universe. Placing your foot on the bottom step, you feel a gentle wave of energy flow through you.

As you travel up the stairs, the vibration of energy softly radiates upward from your feet through your entire body. You begin to feel as if you're floating a few inches above the steps, gliding through emanations of energy, weightless and free, flowing into higher realms of light.

The top of the stairs are shrouded in a soft, white mist. As you enter the mist, it clears, showing a vibrant path shimmering with light. Following the path, you feel the pure white light envelop you with a very pleasant warmth. Breathing in the energy of light, it fills you with a wonderful feeling of peace and harmony.

A few steps ahead, the light illuminates a shimmering building in an open, circular area. The building radiates a special kind of energy.

Stepping into the light, you enter a library that is created entirely with the vibrant energy of the light. Windows reflect rays of universal light everywhere. Vibrations of light form the floors and the walls. Beams of sparkling energy support the arched ceiling; in the center is a domed skylight.

A magical aura surrounds the library; ethereal energies of pure awareness softly reverberate through the vast array of books. A hushed stillness echoes within the library even as it shimmers with energy, with the knowledge contained in the books that fill the shelves and line the walls. As you listen quietly, you hear the books talk in whispers of wisdom and murmurs of mystical knowledge.

The rows of books appear to be endless, as if they go on forever. Walking through the aisles and the alcoves, you see books on every subject imaginable. This library contains all the knowledge that has ever been written or recorded in all the world and the entire universe since the beginning of time, since the beginning of thought.

Running your fingers over the titles of the books, you discover that you can read them within your mind. The books are written in a universal language that you understand easily, just by touching the books or looking at the pictures on the covers.

The words and their images dance into your mind, creating a symphony of sound vibrations, and within the music and the melody, you understand the knowledge inside each book.

Continuing to walk through the library, exploring the light energies of knowledge, you notice another stairway with seven steps that vibrate with a light more dazzling, more brilliant than the light that surrounded the open entrance to the library.

The light shimmers and sparkles with energy as if it's alive. There's a sacred feeling about this light; it seems to contain an essence within itself. The vibrations emanating from this light are filled with images of color that have shape and substance. It looks like a beautiful blur of rainbow colors forming into transparent prisms of light.

Looking into the light, you experience an emotion that goes beyond words and thoughts, and you know that you're about to enter a very sacred space. More than anything else, you want to be part of that light. You want to rush into the light, to become the essence of the light, yet you feel that you might disturb it if you rush, so you wait respectfully and reverently.

The light opens up and invites you in, just as the light at the entrance to the library invited you in. Stepping into the light, you're filled with a feeling of awe and wonderment and pure joy.

Each step of the stairway vibrates in harmony with the colors of a rainbow. Walking slowly, thoughtfully, up the stairs, you pause on every step—feeling the energy, hearing the unique vibration, the tone and hue and experience of each color. Ascending the stairs and absorbing the colors within your body and your mind, you become more and more aware of your soul.

As your awareness expands, you know that you're traveling a stairway that leads you into the true essence of yourself. As you experience your awareness flowing into and through the vibrations of the rainbow, you feel as if you're flying through the energies of muted sounds and colors.

Reaching the top of the stairs, you see that the higher echelon of the library is a loft that contains the written records of every soul's existence, and you know, with a magical sense of inner knowing, that these books vibrate with a light that is unique to every soul and can only be opened and read by that particular soul.

In the center of the loft, you see a table with an open book and a lamp that glows with a luminous light. Next to the table is a comfortable chair. You walk over to the table and look at the book. It seems that the library has been waiting for you to discover it, and the open book has been waiting to be read by you.

Knowing that the book is about your soul, you look at the chapter title that the book is opened to. As you read the words, they begin to vibrate on the page, then to radiate with a soft glow of light, emanating into rays of energy that form images that swirl into your thoughts and sparkle into pictures, opening a special kind of knowing within your mind. Touching the words, your hand begins to vibrate with energy.

You realize how very special this book is. Picking it up, you settle comfortably in the chair. Holding the open book in your hands, your body begins to vibrate with a radiant energy.

You feel as if you're being drawn inside the pages of the book as the words vibrate and resonate in your mind, moving in rhythm and harmony with the flow of spiritual and universal energy.

It feels as if a gentle current of energy is flowing through you, opening up and releasing a higher awareness within. You hear a soft humming sound inside your mind, and as the energy continues to flow through you, you know your spiritual awareness is completely opening up inside you, beginning to surge and soar through every part of your body, mind, and soul.

This is so wonderful, so magical. You smile to yourself, a special smile that you understand deep inside your soul. Hugging the book close to your heart, you know you've found a very special treasure—a book that reveals all your spiritual knowledge, a book that shows you the secrets of your soul.

You read the chapter title again; the words form an image that draws a complete and detailed picture in your mind. You touch the picture in the book, the picture in your mind, feeling the texture of the images. The pictures are solid. The scene is real; it isn't an image that disappears when you blink your eyes.

The words form real pictures. When you read the words, they form pictures that come to life—three-dimensional images that vibrate from the pages into your awareness, into your physical reality—resonating with an energy source that is inspired by the words on the pages.

The book is energy in motion and the words magically transport you into the scene. You're there, inside the picture; you're really there. Looking all around you, you see and feel and experience everything there is to see and feel and experience.

The book is filled with every experience you've ever had or will have, and yet you know you can write and rewrite the pages and paragraphs in any way you choose.

As you look through the pages and read the words that have already been written, your experiences come to life, and you completely understand—with a clarity and knowing that goes beyond words—why they happened and why you chose to experience them.

You feel—with every part of you, with every part of your awareness—the events and emotions inside your experiences as the words draw detailed and descriptive images and scenes within your mind.

The book is timeless as it portrays the pictures of your soul—the essence of your spirit—in your mind, as it speaks to you of the events and emotions in your life, and shows you all the various aspects of all your experiences in every time frame—past, present, and future—and in every dimension of being, in every realm of your awareness.

The book shows you the true reality of you—the true multidimensionality of your soul.

Magical Mist

Walking through the early morning mist, you see a cloud resting gently on the earth as if it is waiting for you. Peering into the cloud, you notice a chair that is made of the cloud itself. The cloud invites you on a magical journey to go anywhere you want to go and to explore anything you want you experience.

As you sit in this chair, you notice that it is the most comfortable chair you have ever sat in. It surrounds you and completely supports you, fitting its shape and form around you, and you feel completely safe.

As you sink deeply into its cushiony softness, it begins to lift you off the ground, and you glide through the air, higher and higher, weightless, unrestrained by gravity, completely free and light, floating easily through the air, going as slowly or as quickly as you wish, enjoying the view.

Feel the delight of gliding through the air freely and effortlessly, utterly silent, floating through the gentle breeze like a feather on the wind.

The sky is any way that you would like it to be: it is the deepest, clearest blue, or the starriest, blackest night. You can create a rainbow sky or anything else that pleases you.

The sun and the moon are smiling upon you, welcoming you with their warmth and light, illuminating your magical journey.

You know that you can direct the course of the wind to take you anywhere you wish to go, and the cloud will acquiesce to your merest wisp of a thought, taking you instantly there and waiting patiently for you to explore and then to return to the cloud to travel again somewhere else and to explore other things.

Travel anywhere you wish, perhaps to a far planet or inside your own body, to another plane of awareness or another place on earth. Let yourself go wherever you wish and spend as much time there as you desire.

Sometime and somewhere in your journey, you will meet two wonderful beings. One is a new friend who will help you understand the significance of your journey; the other is a very wise counselor who will offer you guidance and wisdom.

Travel now to anywhere you wish, and when you are done, the cloud will return you to where you began your magical journey.

Realms of Reality

This is a completely self-guided meditation, a very special inner journey. Allow an image or a dream or a memory to form in your mind. Accept and acknowledge whatever appears in the way that it shows itself. Let it come into full focus and form.

Explore and experience every aspect of it. Know that it is real and true and valid. Guided by your inner knowing, let your mind show you the many wonders inside yourself; let your mind share with you the secrets of your soul and the true realities of your multidimensional self.

As the image, dream, or memory—or perhaps what you perceive as an entirely new experience—appears in your mind, you may experience an intense feeling of déjà vu—of having been there before or of having experienced the scene before, but without quite remembering where or when. You have an absolute knowing that it really happened, but you're not sure if it occurred in a physical place, or somewhere inside your mind, or perhaps in another realm of your reality.

Clearly pinpoint the image, thought, feeling, scene, event or experience, and place by completely focusing on and sensing the vibrations and energies associated with it. Keep in mind that time and space are fluid in this deeper realm of reality, this inner dimension of your mind.

Immerse yourself totally in your meditation. Go with the flow of your thoughts and feelings. Center in on what your mind shares with you and shows you. See everything there is to see and know everything there is to know.

Special Star

It's a beautiful, clear, moonlit evening. Gazing up at the millions of stars hanging gracefully in the universe in perfect symmetry, seeing their sparkling, radiant emanations of light as they shine brightly, you marvel that their light shines upon the earth, shines upon you. You wonder how this light is bright enough for you to see through the blackness, through the void of space.

Knowing that the light you see originated many thousands of years ago, perhaps eons ago, you begin to wonder about the origins of the stars. You wonder how they came into being, how they sustain themselves, why they were created, and for what purpose. You sense that there is a greater purpose than simply to light up the heavens and revolve in seemingly endless circles.

You begin to wonder about your source, your origin, how you came into being, how you began life, and what initiated your creation. You wonder if your soul was born the same way the stars were born, and how long your soul has existed. You wonder about your purpose; you know that you have a greater purpose in life than to merely exist as a physical being and to go around in seemingly endless circles.

One star catches your attention as it twinkles brightly in the sky, shining its light upon you. You feel an affinity with this star. It seems to be a very special star, calling to you and inviting you into its light, asking you to travel the light of this star to its source. With that thought, you sense yourself traveling through the sky, through the infinite universe on the energy of light from the star, going back in time as the light draws you to its source.

Thoughts and images begin to race through your mind, and you wonder if you are also being drawn toward the source of what you think might be your beginning of life, might be the beginning of you—the birth of your soul.

Zooming on the vibration of light, you are going faster and faster, traveling at the speed of light and even faster through space, seeing, knowing, remembering every experience you've ever had in every moment of life, as a physical being and as a spiritual being, in every form that your soul has ever been in. You remember every multidimensional aspect of your soul, in all of its many vibrations and expressions.

Looking at all the stars and the planets that surround you, you remember living on some of them. Your memories are very clear and vivid. Flashes of recognition zip in and out of your awareness quickly, yet you have full comprehension and complete understanding of every experience, every event and emotion, every second of every life, and you see with a clarity that goes way beyond human comprehension.

You're so very far above the earth now. Looking down at the earth—the beautiful green and blue globe that you call home for the present moment—you remember and reexperience every moment of every life you've had on earth.

Continuing to hurtle through the universe, through space, you realize that it isn't a black void as you first thought. It is filled with a life and vibrancy and energy that is continuous and ever-changing.

At last you reach the star that beckoned to you, the special star that invited you to travel its light, to see and experience its source. This star shares the knowledge of its birth and its source of light with you. Walking around this star, seeing and knowing its origin and life-force, its energy vibration, you begin to wonder again about the birth of your soul.

Was the birth of your soul similar to the birth of this star? Or maybe your soul was born on this star, and that's why you could travel its light source so easily. Or did seeing the origin and birth of this star simply remind you of the birth of your soul?

As you watch the beginnings—the birth of this star—memories of your origin begin to come into your mind. Vague at first, they then become clearer and more focused as you center your awareness and attention on them, and you see and remember the beginnings and birth of your soul, the beginning of your light in the universe.

Knowing and experiencing the birth of this star, you recognize that its beginnings are similar to your soul's beginnings. With your remembrance, you travel to a special place in the universe to reunite and reconnect with your spiritual source. It's a dimension of *being-ness* where your soul was born and where you return, time and time again, to your source to renew yourself—your spiritual essence and awareness, your light—after every lifetime, after every existence, wherever you have lived before.

You experience a sense of timelessness as your soul's multidimensional awareness opens up completely. It's as if the star you explored exists just as much in the future as in the past, and its light is never-ending and always becoming.

You know, too, that your soul is timeless, and that it has always existed and will always exist. And though you remember your birth—your soul's beginnings, the creation of your spiritual essence when your awareness was born—you realize that there is no death, no end, that your soul is continuous and exists forever, that your light shines brightly, both in this world and in other worlds, and that the light of your soul goes on forever.

But then doubt begins to set in. This is only a thought, a muse in your mind, an imaginary trip, an inner journey—or is it much more than that? Is it real? It seemed very real when you were remembering and experiencing it.

And what about the multidimensionality of your soul? Have you really lived on other planets and stars? How could your soul be born if it has always existed? Pondering your thoughts, your mind going around in circles, returning to the memory and moment of your soul's birth—the origin of your spiritual awareness—you wonder again about your purpose.

Still wondering about all of this and whether it's real, you blink your eyes and gaze up at the special star in the universe that shared its source with you and invited you within its light.

Seeing its sparkling, radiant emanations of light as it shines brightly in the universe, you marvel at the light of the star and at the light of your soul as it shines brightly, sharing its light with the earth.

Whirling White Light

Imagine and know that you have the power to command and direct the energy of the universe. Begin this meditation by imagining circles and spirals of white light that softly and gently vibrate around your physical body, moving slowly up and down in a flowing motion.

Do this for a few moments to get into the flow of energy, to feel it around you, and to center your awareness within these whirling beams of white light. You may begin to feel a pleasant sensation of warmth, and you may hear a humming or a buzzing sound. This is a sign that you're accessing astral energy.

Keep in mind that you are in control at all times. You can speed up or slow down or completely stop the vibrations of energy as you choose. The energy will always feel pleasant, and you will always feel comfortable with everything you experience.

Increase the vibrations and the circular, spherical motion all around you so that the energy of this whirling white light becomes very intense and rapid. While you're doing this, you may experience other sounds and images as your consciousness travels into and through higher planes of energy and awareness.

Perhaps you'll hear beautiful tones of harmonious music or the sound of tinkling bells, or you may experience traveling through various shapes, such as a tunnel or clouds or luminous mists, or see rainbow-colored hues and lights, and angelic beings or spiritual guides and masters. The sights, sounds, and feelings are a sign that you're accessing higher vibrations of ethereal energy.

As you continue to intensify and accelerate the vibrations of energy and light, you may also hear the sound of wind roaring in your ears and experience the feeling of it moving all around you. This is normal and natural; there's an incredible amount of power and energy here that is expressing itself. The sounds and feelings are a sign that you're accessing ever-increasing vibrations of universal energy.

Begin to bring these vibrations of powerful white light energies inside you so that they are vibrating within you and through you as well as all around you. Breathe them inside you or simply absorb them within you, much as you experience the warmth of sunlight on your skin as it permeates your body. Gradually, be and become one with the light.

As you soak up the energies of the light within you, it balances and blends your physical and spiritual energies with universal energy to cleanse and purify your body, mind, and spirit, and to bring your physical consciousness into harmony with your spiritual awareness.

As you bring these whirling circles and spirals of white light inside you, and you are within the center of this energy vortex of universal vibrations, you experience a wonderful, super healing on a physical level and a shower of awareness on a spiritual level—a sunburst of universal enlightenment.

As the light permeates deep within you, it clears all the cobwebs from your mind, cleanses the toxins from your body and your thoughts, frees your feelings and emotions from negativity, and opens up your full awareness of your true spiritual nature.

As these circles and spirals of white light continue to encircle you and to vibrate within you, you realize how powerful they are—how powerful you are—and you simultaneously realize that this same energy resides in a reservoir deep inside you, welling up and releasing the spiritual power you have within you.

You sense and feel and know that the essence of your soul is intricately intertwined and interwoven with the universal vibrations of white light, and that your soul is completely in tune with and vibrates to the same energies as universal light.

Explore and enjoy these whirling circles and spirals of white light energy. Experience the cleansing and healing in your body, mind, and spirit, and the complete opening up of your awareness.

When you're ready to end this meditation, gradually decrease the vibrations of energy, feeling and sensing the energies around you and within you slowing down to a physical level.

There is a knowingness deep inside you that white light is always instantly available to you and that there are many practical and metaphysical applications for this energy; it works for any positive reason at any time.

This loving white light energy is your spiritual birthright to use in any way you desire in your physical life. It always works for the highest good of all.

It is also a reminder that you are truly a spiritual being of light, here to share your awareness and knowledge, and to allow your essence— the light of your soul—to shine brightly in the physical world, to radiate and emanate in and through every thought and feeling you have, touching everyone you meet and everything you do, influencing all aspects of every experience you have.

Planetary Peace Project

Your inner journeys have brought you to a still, quiet, peaceful place within you—a special, sacred place filled with light—where you remember your soul's natural vibration: a vibration of light, love, joy, peace, and harmony.

Feel this vibration completely within yourself, with every part of your body, mind, and soul. Breathe it inside you; allow it to become part of you. The feeling is so filled with pure joy that words cannot adequately describe it, yet you completely feel it and know it within yourself.

This vibration of spiritual knowing and pure peace has so much joy and wisdom and beauty within it that it naturally desires to express itself.

In this special, sacred place within you, within the center of your soul, the very core of your being, you have always, in every moment of your life, shared your vibrations with the world and the universe, even though you may not have been fully aware of it.

You have always come from a loving, white light place within your heart, mind, and soul. Because you are a spiritual being, born from a divine spark of love, you could not do otherwise, even though at times physical illusions may have prevented your clear seeing of the whole picture and of knowing the reasons for your experiences and actions. Yet your soul was ever-evolving, following its path of inner knowing directed by its inner source to its ultimate destiny—that of love and light.

Now that you've reawakened and remembered your spiritual awareness and the light within you, you know that you can increase your power to share your vibrations of love, peace, and harmony throughout the world and the universe by joining with others who have also awakened to this awareness.

Desiring to share your vibrations with the world, you draw into your life like-minded people—kindred spirits—who are also aware of their soul's natural vibrations, people who have awakened to their spiritual mission to share the light of their knowledge and the vibrations of love, joy, peace, and harmony in their own special, unique, individual way throughout the world.

As you join with this group—whether you're physically connected by geography or universally connected in mind and spirit—to share peace and love with everyone, you know that every soul who is now experiencing life on earth is truly a spiritual being of light, just as you are, and that their spark of divine love is ever-present, sometimes waiting only for a way-shower—for your light to shine upon them to illuminate the light that is within them.

As these peaceful vibrations—both from within yourself and from like-minded people—surround you, you are joined by light-beings from other planets in the universe who have the same desire to share their vibrations of love, peace, and harmony with the earth and throughout the universe, just as you do.

As you become connected with other spiritually-awakened people and light-beings through your soul's awareness, you know that your thoughts, feelings, and actions, and the way you express and manifest them in your life through all your many experiences, create vibrations of loving, peaceful energy everywhere as they simultaneously create beautiful, loving reverberations and ripples of peace and harmony throughout the earth and the universe.

In your daily life, simply feel your soul's natural vibration of energy within you. Allow it to grow and expand, both inward—bringing you feelings of joy and happiness and peace within yourself—and outward, as you share your vibrations of love, peace, joy, and harmony with the world and the universe.

Mystical Moonlight

It's a beautiful, warm, moonlit evening, and you're enjoying a quiet stroll by a lake. Stopping to look at the reflection of the moon on the water, you notice how it shimmers with a luminescent light, almost as if it's alive. A calm, gentle breeze ripples across the surface, inspiring a magical, mystical sense of awareness within you.

Walking to the edge of the water, admiring the beauty of the reflection of moonlight on the water, and enjoying the sense of harmony that it brings forth within you, you notice how the light shimmers with an effervescent energy. Stepping into the warm, shallow water, you feel the softly swirling effervescence gently bubbling and radiating around your feet.

Bending down, you scoop up handfuls of the warm water, letting it run through your fingers, noticing the tingling in your hands. As you splash the water over your face and body, bathing in the light from the moon reflecting on the water, you feel your hands and body become warmer and energized with the tingling effervescence of the water.

Joyfully, with carefree abandon, you play in the water. As you splash the water over your body and in circles all around you, you feel your body begin to tingle and vibrate with a sense of energy and vitality that you've experienced before, a long time ago when your spirit was free and filled with light, and you realize that you're bathing in the divine light of the universe—the light of your soul.

As this remembrance reawakens within you, you look up at the sky, the infinite universe, and you breathe in the light of the sparkling stars that combine their light with the light emanating and radiating from the moon. You know that this universal light reflects your soul's divine essence.

You feel a beautiful, wonderful feeling of radiant health and harmony within your body, mind, and spirit, freeing you and opening you up more and more to your true spiritual nature—that of a divine, powerful, spiritual being who has only taken up a temporary residence here on earth.

A Gift from the Gods

A gift box falls from the sky, from the universe, landing softly beside you. Looking inside, you see that it appears to be empty, but as you peer closer, you notice that a small, slim book appears, seemingly from out of nowhere. Opening it, you notice that the pages are blank, but you're determined to decode the messages that you know are written there.

Flipping through the pages, you begin to see faint, barely visible images of words. As you read the images, they pop up into pictures, much like a child's storybook. You notice that the pictures fill in with colors and details, and become vivid and descriptive the more you place your attention and awareness within them. The pictures tell you the story of your life and show you the many different experiences of your soul.

With every page you turn, the book grows in volume and size as more pages are added, showing you the many different aspects of your soul, and the many avenues and directions it has traveled—the paths it has followed and the journeys it has taken.

It seems as if the book is writing itself as you read it, but you also know that you have the power to edit and revise this book, to write and rewrite it any way that you want to.

It is both fiction and nonfiction, containing all the facts and the many faces and facets of your soul. It describes—in vibrant, illuminating images and words—the dearest and most private wishes and hopes in your heart. It offers you stories, parables, and proverbs—some symbolic and some literal.

This beautiful book shows you many insights and inner knowings as it offers you images and inner journeys. It contains possibilities and probabilities, and shares with you various imprints of experiences yet to be and offers you choices as to how you'd like to shape and sculpt the future.

It invites you to listen and look within your mind, heart, and soul, into your imagination to write and rewrite the past, present, and future—to change your feelings and experiences with a slight stroke of your thoughts and a soft touch of your emotions.

This magical, mystical book is a gift from the gods—a treasure of truth—given to you to open up and read your spiritual knowledge, your inner knowing, and to write the story of your soul.

Charismatic Cave

It is early twilight on a warm summer night. As you are walking down a gently-winding path, you come upon a small stream with a bridge over it. As you walk over the bridge, you are met by a guide. Perhaps it is your inner self who appears to guide you on a special journey through seven rainbow-colored gates.

Your guide takes your hand, and you walk with him or her, completely trusting, knowing that your guide is an old and dear friend that you have traveled with before.

Your guide leads you to an entrance to a cave where you feel a flow of cool, moist air coming from the darkness, and you smell the damp scent of the earth. Surrounded by a nurturing, comforting sensation, you follow your guide into the cave where you stop in front of a glowing red light.

A beautiful, melodious voice whispers to you in your mind, telling you that this is the first of seven gates that you will encounter on your journey. You are told that at each one you will leave behind a worldly attachment of your choice—perhaps a role you play, a prized possession, a personality characteristic, an attitude, or an emotion or feeling that you hold for yourself or another, a belief, an expectation, or some other attachment.

You are easily able to choose which one you will leave here. As you do this, the gate takes on a particular shape that is symbolic to you. Notice what shape it takes. Once you let go of your attachment, you are able to step through the gate and continue on your journey through the cave with your guide.

In the distance you see a glowing orange light signifying the second gate. As you approach, the light seems to envelop you, and again you are instructed to leave behind a worldly attachment. You take a moment to decide what you will leave behind. When you do, the symbolic shape of this gate appears to you. You move through it with ease and continue on your journey.

The third light you see in the cave is yellow, and you are immediately surrounded by its intensity. You sense an awareness within its vibration—the beginning of an opening up of your inner knowledge. You are again requested to leave behind one of your earthly attachments. The decision is a bit difficult, but you are able to decide, and the symbolic shape of this third gate is revealed to you. You move through it effortlessly and proceed along your path.

The fourth light you see is a healing green radiance that permeates your entire being and brings a sense of peace and calm. It affirms to you that you are on the right path, and when you are asked to leave another worldly attachment behind, you quickly decide which one so that you may continue your journey through the cave. As before, the symbol of the fourth gate is magically revealed to you with your choice, and you step through this gate with anticipation.

The fifth light you see is a brilliant blue spiral that encircles you with its energy and also asks you to leave an attachment behind in order to enter the next gate on your journey. The choice seems more difficult, but you are able to leave something here, and as you do, you feel much lighter in body and spirit. The symbolic shape of the fifth gate is revealed to you, and once again you feel the presence of your guide leading you on your journey through this cave.

The sixth area of light you see is a deep, velvet-like, violet-blue light that wraps itself around you like a cloak of inner knowing—an intuitive awareness—and requests that another earthly attachment be left behind. You gladly choose what to leave here, beginning to have a clearer sense of what awaits you. The shape of the sixth gate is revealed, and as you slowly step through it you know that you're opening up your spiritual essence, and you have a joyful feeling of anticipation.

Though it is dark in this cave, you move forward, trusting your guide, adjusting with all your senses to its blackness, to the seeming void that you are experiencing, yet you know somewhere within you that this void is filled with light.

Now your guide asks you to stop for a moment. You remain in the blackness for what seems to be a long time, taking this opportunity to just *be* because you are now free from your worldly distractions and can experience the simple essence of who you are. You find the experience of seeing and knowing yourself in your essence to be empowering and quite profound.

As your eyes become adjusted to the darkness, you begin to perceive, using your senses at first and then using your eyes, a violet pinpoint of light glowing in the distance. It gradually moves closer, as though it is trying to reach out to you. You sense that it is full of goodness and love, and you start to see a transparent image of your own body beginning to appear. The silhouette is filmy and smoke-like, ethereal, but it definitely has the size and shape of your body.

Observe this body forming from where you are standing in the darkness. Slowly, it becomes more real as it begins to take on a solid shape, yet it is still transparent as if it is made up of many tiny energy vibrations of violet light. The light continues to fill your ethereal body, and, at the same time, the violet light begins to merge with a brilliant, dazzling white light; it becomes more solid and substantial.

Although it is still made of light, the solid material begins to predominate, and your guide indicates that you can join with it whenever you are ready. You reach out and tentatively touch it. It is incredibly strong and calm; its energy is immense.

Your essence, discovered in the darkness, easily merges with your light-body image. The effervescent sensation you feel is so absolutely wonderful that words can't truly describe it.

All of a sudden you realize that it is this body shape that is the symbol of the seventh gate and that by joining with it, you have already gone through the gate and are now making your way upward out of the darkness.

Slowly, but with a newfound lightness and power, you move up out of the cave, enjoying your light-body and being the essence of your true, spiritual self. It feels free and light, yet grounded and centered at the same time. You take a few deep breaths to more fully experience this wondrous part of yourself.

Your light-body continues to feel more and more solid, more physical, as you emerge from the cave of darkness until it is almost, but not exactly, the same vibration as your physical body. It is lighter and now free of the cares and worldly attachments you have left behind in this charismatic cave of yourself that is now filled with your inner light.

As you step out of the cave, take your time to reflect on your spiritual essence that you have experienced and merged with on your journey. If you'd like, your guide—whom you now recognize as your inner self, as the beautiful, melodious voice that whispered to you at the beginning of your journey—can explain any part of your voyage and answer all the questions you may have, showing you the symbolic meanings for each gate you went through and helping you to understand the meanings of the attachments that you chose to let go of.

Take some time to just *be* the light-being that you have become, that you have always been, but perhaps haven't always remembered or recognized. Enjoy the light and energy that comprises the essence of your spirit—the essence of who you truly are.

Beautiful Balloon

Imagine a big, beautiful, colorful hot-air balloon. You've always wanted to ride in one, and you climb into the basket, making yourself comfortable as it is about to be launched from a large, open field. As the balloon lifts gently off the ground, you feel your mind and spirit lifting into the air, becoming free and unencumbered by cares and worries. As the balloon lifts up higher and higher, your mind expands into a wonderful feeling of joy and exhilaration.

You peer over the side of the basket, seeing all the sights below you and listening to the gentle floating of the balloon through the air. You feel the soft, gentle breeze as the wind moves the balloon on its journey—on your journey above yourself, above the earth.

The sunlight shimmers all around you. Looking up, you notice that there isn't a cloud in the deep-blue sky. You see a full moon coming up over the horizon even though it's still afternoon. This perspective of seeing the earth below you and the universe above you helps you to realize how expansive and free your mind is, and you know that your spirit can rise above yourself at any time you desire.

The balloon floats very slowly over open meadows and fields, passing rivers and streams, hills and valleys. Your balloon is now drifting over a beautiful sapphire-blue lake. You feel a cool sensation on your skin as you drift farther across the lake, and you breathe in the freshness of the air that surrounds you. You see the reflection of the moon as it rises higher in the afternoon sky, next to the reflection of the balloon.

As the afternoon progresses, your balloon continues to drift. Your thoughts and feelings float peacefully through your mind. As dusk begins to softly fall, a few stars can be seen in the sky in the early twilight.

You watch the sun as it approaches the horizon; it looks like a perfect golden disk. It seems so close that you feel you could almost reach out and touch it. As it begins to sink slowly and gracefully below the horizon, a sunset appears, radiating rays of gentle light that color the entire universe in a beautiful splendor of golds and oranges. The sunset surrounds you and fills you with awe of the universe. As you stare in wonder at the sunset, it fades slowly.

The sky is filled with the beautiful, luminescent light of the full moon, and other stars begin to appear. The moon is lifting higher in the sky as you float along in your beautiful, magical balloon. Now the stars become very clear with a dazzling brightness that surrounds you. Different stars have different patterns as they flicker with a rhythm that gives movement to the night sky.

You feel a complete oneness with the universe as you drift along, absorbing all of the rhythms and vibrations of light. You feel in perfect harmony with all of creation, and it's as if your entire life is centered around this moment. You feel as if you're centered within a beautiful dream, and yet you're completely awake and aware. It's as if your soul has awakened from a long sleep, and the dream is real—it's a reality that you enjoy with every part of you.

As your soul awakens and your mind becomes clear, the night sky becomes beautiful patterns of coral and pink and orange light that appear over the horizon where the sun is about to rise. You see the glorious, vibrant colors of the sunrise light up the early morning sky, and you're in awe of the magic that the light brings to both the earth and the universe, bathing them in a brilliant golden light and warmth.

You experience a oneness with the sunrise in a special way that your soul completely understands; it's as if you are part of the sunrise, and the light of the sun is the same light that shines brightly within you.

Your balloon is now drifting over a beautiful green forest as the sun continues to rise in the sky, illuminating every part of the earth and the universe, illuminating every part of your mind and soul.

You see brightly-colored birds in the tops of the trees and hear their sounds very clearly as they chirp their welcoming songs to the sunrise. Your soul begins to sing in harmony with the light, with the dawn of a new day, with the dawn of your awareness completely opening up within you.

A new day is beginning for you, and, as your balloon drifts back to the field where you started, your mind and your soul feel energized and refreshed by all the beautiful moments you've experienced as your balloon settles to a soft, easy landing in the field.

Meandering Meadow

You're walking in a magical meadow. It's a warm day, and you feel a gentle breeze on your face. You hear birds singing in the nearby forest. You begin to walk toward the forest. It seems magical and mystical, and you wonder about its mysteries.

You feel compelled to follow the path that you see through the trees. As you walk through the forest, you notice that it is welcoming and protective. The trees are tall and majestic, rising up toward the sky. They beckon to you as if they want to share the secrets of the earth and the universe with you.

You sense an air of magic here, and, as you progress through the forest along the path, you see a clearing up ahead. As you approach the clearing, there is a beautiful light—shafts of sunlight—filtering through the tops of the trees.

When you arrive at the clearing, you see a shallow pond in front of you; the light is reflecting a spectrum of colors on the surface. You become absorbed by the shimmering, sparkling colors that play on the surface of the pond. The more you look at them, the more vivid the patterns and colors become.

At first, the colors are in tiny fragments of blue and green, and they move in small swirls and gentle ripples, caressed by a soft, airy breeze. As you look at them, the patterns of color begin to dance in your mind as they turn into a mixture of dark blue and violet.

The various hues seem to have a rhythm of their own, and as you watch the colors, you begin to hear soft, beautiful music. The music has a cadence and clarity in tune with the rhythm and patterns of the dancing, sparkling colors. You begin to experience a feeling of supreme wonder and happiness as the patterns and the music create a magical melody inside your mind.

As the music continues, you begin to feel as if the chords and sounds they make are softly touching the skin all over your body with gentle tingles of energy. You feel the music with each rhythm passing around your body, through your body, and into your body.

As you resonate with the music, it begins to heal you. You experience a sense of health and harmony and well-being that transcends anything you have ever felt before; you feel as if you are part of the music. You feel a oneness with the world around you, and a sense of completeness within yourself.

You notice that the pond flows into a softly-swirling stream of water. Peacefully, you begin to walk alongside the stream through the forest with a song in your heart.

In order to go farther, you see that you have to take off your shoes and wade across a shallow part of the stream to follow the path on the other side. As you wade through the water, you feel the soft, silky, muddy bottom between your toes and the cool water around your feet. The stream has a magical effect upon you, and you experience a wonderful sense of well-being and happiness.

Stopping and bending down, you dip your hand into the stream and take a drink of the crystal-clear water. It tastes so fresh and clean that you dip your hand in repeatedly to drink from the magic stream. You feel a wonderful strength come over you as you drink the water, and you know that the magic water will benefit your health. You experience a sense of rejuvenation and youth that you haven't felt for a long time.

When you reach the other side of the pond, you continue along the path that leads through the forest. Looking farther ahead at the path, you see that as the forest ends, the path opens up and leads you into a field filled with beautiful flowers of many colors.

As you walk into the flower-covered field, you notice that the scents of the flowers are so sweet, so perfect, that you can taste them as you breathe in their delightful, delicate essence and aroma. You lean over several individual flowers and deeply inhale their fragrance as you admire their beauty. The flowers give you a wonderful feeling of pleasure and joy, of peace and harmony. You walk through the field of flowers very slowly, enjoying every moment.

At the far side of the field, you notice that the path gently slopes up to the top of a large hill. You decide to follow the path to the top of the hill so you can look at all the wondrous things you have seen and experienced during your walk through this magical, meandering meadow.

Reaching the top of the hill, you look over the field of flowers, the glorious garden that you enjoyed so completely with every part of you; they make a beautiful picture in your mind. You pause for a moment to make the picture clearer and more defined, so that you can easily remember it.

There are so many colors and flowers that fill your mind with lovely sensations. Looking back over the forest, you see the wonderful, magical pond that gave you so much pleasure with its sparkling colors and shimmering lights, with its sounds and patterns, and the rhythm of its music. You see the stream of gently swirling water that offered you health and rejuvenation, and you remember all these experiences clearly as they replay in your mind.

You decide to return to the meadow where you began your walk, promising yourself that you'll remember everything you saw and felt and experienced.

You notice that the path continues down the hill on the other side and returns you to the meadow where you began your walk, and you realize that the end of this journey is really the beginning, that you are traveling a timeless, never-ending path that offers you enjoyment and enlightenment with every step you take.

When you arrive at the meadow, you feel as if your entire spirit has been uplifted, and that you have taken a wonderful, magical, mystical walk through a meandering meadow that brought you back in tune with yourself, in rhythm and harmony with your essence, your soul.

Center of the Sunrise

Sunrises hold a promise of a new and wonderful discovery—the dawn of a new beginning, the dawn of a new light beginning within you. Explore and experience the light within yourself as you travel in your mind into and beyond the center of the sunrise, as you completely remember your inner knowing and rediscover your spiritual knowledge.

Imagine . . .

It's only moments before dawn. It's a beautiful summer morning, and you're outside enjoying the beginning of a new day. You feel a gentle, warm breeze and smell the fresh scent of the morning air. You hear birds chirping in the distance, and the sound is muted and pleasant as they welcome the dawn of a new day.

Looking around, you see a few trees, and the ground is covered with grass. You feel like taking off your shoes and walking barefoot in the grass. It feels like velvet beneath your feet, and, as you walk, you feel free and happy, enjoying the beginning of a brand-new day.

You know that there's a beach nearby because you can hear the sound of the waves, and you think you'd enjoy the sunrise even more if you were at the beach. You begin to walk toward the beach and now you can feel the sand beneath your feet; it feels pleasantly warm and cushions you as you walk.

Sitting on the beach and watching the waves as they gently touch the shore, you feel a wonderful sense of peace and harmony within yourself and all around you. Listening to the ebb and flow of the tide relaxes you completely. Breathing in deeply, you feel perfectly content, at one with yourself and with the world around you.

Looking across the water, you have a clear view of the horizon as the water seemingly touches the sky. There are a few clouds just above the horizon, and you notice that they're tinged with the early colors of dawn: pale orange at first, then the pale orange blends into a beautiful mixture of coral and pink as the first rays of sunlight color the bottom of the clouds.

The beauty and misty softness of the colors inspire a sense of awe and wonderment inside you, and you recognize that you're seeing more than the colors of a new day; you're seeing the colors of a new beginning.

You notice that the sky is getting lighter. As the light from the sun begins to shine behind the clouds, you see the first rays of the sunrise come over the horizon, and the light is reflected and mirrored on the water.

The light of this sunrise emanates a wonderful feeling of energy, and you sense that this sunrise is very special; it's magical and has a mystical aura and ambiance about it. Turning your face up to the sun, you breathe in the light.

The warmth and light of the sun envelops you as you breathe it inside your mind and your body. It fills your entire body and your mind with pure energy and awareness, gently touching every nerve, every muscle, and every fiber of your body.

You feel your body and your mind vibrating in harmony with the warmth and light of the sun, with the energy of awareness. As you experience the sunrise with every part of you, you feel drawn into it.

The early colors of dawn begin to change into the golden color of the sun, the color of knowledge. Somewhere within yourself, you realize that you are the colors of dawn. You are the colors of the sunrise.

Just as the water mirrored the beginning of the sunrise, you know that the sunrise mirrored within your mind is a reflection of your spiritual awareness, opening up within you, reawakening you to the knowledge within yourself.

The sunlight sparkles and shimmers on the water, reflecting the light. Centering your awareness into the sunrise, you notice that it becomes brighter, illuminating every part of your mind, filling your mind and your spirit with pure enlightenment. You know that the sunrise is within you and that you are the sunrise.

The sun is above the horizon now, and as the sun continues to rise in the sky, you rise with it—higher and higher. The feeling is exhilarating, and you feel more alive and awake and aware than you've ever felt before.

There's a special place that you know of, a magical place that you've just remembered is beyond the colors of dawn, beyond the spectrum of the sunrise. As you go into and through and beyond the light of the sunrise, you enter that special and most magical place within yourself.

It feels as if you're coming home, as if you're returning to yourself. You know you've been here before in this sacred place inside your soul. You've always known the way to this most special and magical place.

You see the sun beginning to rise in the center of yourself and a pure white light—a light brighter than the sunrise—enters into every part of your mind. You feel this light, this energy of spiritual awareness, vibrating inside your body, your mind, and your soul.

You experience a feeling of total joy as you completely open yourself up to this magical energy of spiritual awareness and enlightenment, knowing that it has always been part of you.

This pure white light opens your awareness to the truth of your spiritual essence and knowledge. As the light becomes brighter and brighter within you, you become more and more aware of your inner spiritual knowledge—knowledge that is infinite and goes beyond what words can describe.

You know that this light is the light of your soul, the light of your spiritual essence vibrating all around you and within you. As you breathe in the pure and positive energy of the light, you fully absorb the spiritual energy within yourself, knowing that your spiritual enlightenment is completely opening up inside you as you become more aware and awake than ever before.

As you accept the light that is radiating from within the center of the sunrise, from within the center of your being—your soul—you become fully aware of your true spiritual nature and you know that *you are the essence of light that shines upon the earth.*

The light within you becomes brighter as the sun continues to rise. Your spiritual knowledge and the awareness of your true nature is interwoven with the rays of sunshine, with the colors of a new day, a new beginning. Your inner knowing becomes clearer and brighter at every moment as you experience and enjoy the sunrise, as you experience enlightenment within your mind and your spirit.

You see a golden sun ray that emanates from the sunrise, a golden sun ray that emanates from you. You notice how it originates from the sun and from you, and how it travels from its source to gently touch the earth and to light the way of a beautiful new day.

You notice that this sun ray sparkles on the water and shines on the beach where you watched the dawn begin, where you enjoyed the beginning of the sunrise. Travel with that golden sun ray onto the beach where you watched the dawning of the light within you.

You're sitting on the beach again, and you see that the sun is completely above the horizon, above the clouds. The colors are different now; the clouds that reflected the early colors of dawn now reflect the color of gold, the color of the sun, and the color of knowledge.

The sky is a very bright blue, and even as you look at the clouds that are golden, they change to a pure white as if they've absorbed the light of the sunrise.

You look over the water and notice how it sparkles and shimmers, mirroring and reflecting the light from the sun. And you know that the light of your soul shines brightly within you and is mirrored and reflected in the world around you.

You feel the warmth of the sun and the gentle breeze. You smell the scent of the morning air and hear the sound of birds chirping in the distance as they welcome the light.

You smile up at the sun, knowing that you've remembered your true spiritual nature and rediscovered your soul's knowledge within yourself on the journey you've just taken beyond the center of the sunrise.

Afterword

The Inner Journey Continues . . .

The meditations and visualizations you've experienced in this book are just the beginning. As you continue to meditate, to journey into and explore your inner worlds to see and know all that is within your heart, mind, and soul, and you open yourself up to your inner spiritual knowing and expand your awareness more and more, reaching above the horizons of your physical world into the universe, you'll discover the many joys and riches and treasures and freedom that meditating offers you.

As you explore and journey into and through your insights and inner knowing, you'll discover that the full opening up of your awareness is like the dawn of a new beginning that offers a promise of many new and wonderful adventures and discoveries.

Your insights and inner knowing—your spiritual awareness—are reflected and mirrored in every experience in your life as you journey upon this path that you're now traveling—a magical, mystical path in your mind that leads you into the light of your soul.

As you continue on your inner journeys, many treasures and rewards await you with every step you take. Spiritual knowledge is the most wonderful treasure of all because this knowledge leads you to the true awareness of who you are and empowers you to express your insights and inner knowing in all your thoughts, feelings, and experiences.

As you stretch your mind and soul beyond the borders of your physical and mental worlds into multidimensional realms and realities of both the earth and the universe, you'll realize that you are ever so much more than your physical self. Keep in mind that once upon a time, somewhere inside your soul, you knew all there is to know. All you need to do is to remember and bring forth your spiritual knowledge into your life.

You'll see and actualize your spiritual self—that very special, sacred part of you—that is reflected in every aspect of your day-to-day activities, in every thought, feeling, and experience you have in your life, and you'll reawaken to your true spiritual nature, to the energy essence of yourself—the universal light-being that you truly are. Travel lightly on your journeys.

Remember that the joy is in the journey.